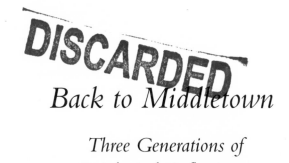

Back to Middletown

Three Generations of
Sociological Reflections

RITA CACCAMO

Stanford University Press
Stanford, California

Originally published in Italian in 1992 under the title
Ritorno a Middletown. La provincia americana dai Lynd agli anni '90
1992 Bulzoni Editore

Stanford University Press
Stanford, California
© 2000 by the Board of Trustees
of the Leland Stanford Junior University

Printed in the United States of America
CIP data appear at the end of the book

Contents

Back to Middletown

ARTHUR J. VIDICH

Foreword

PUBLISHED IN 1927, Robert and Helen Merrell Lynds' *Middletown: A Study in Modern American Culture* became a sociological reference point for the quality of life in the United States during the twenties. The Lynds' *Middletown in Transition*, a 1937 restudy of the same community, now known to be Muncie, Indiana, described a community and its leaders in the throes of the Great Depression, providing a second reference point on community values in the midst of crisis. Achieving the status of cultural benchmarks, these two books became the subject of an enormous secondary literature on Muncie/Middletown, including hundreds of essays, articles, dissertations, monographs, a restudy by Theodore Caplow published in two volumes, *Middletown Families: Fifty Years of Change and Continuity* (1982) and *All Faithful People* (1983), and a series of six documentary films shot in Muncie and available with teaching notes for sociology students. This burgeoning sociological and historical documentation of life in Muncie is collected and housed in the Center for Middletown Studies at Ball State University, a veritable data bank that also includes Robert S. Lynd's papers, secondary publications and foreign communications about Middletown studies, and the manuscripts, letters, and diaries of Helen Merrell Lynd. Nowhere in the United States is there a comparable archive on a single American community that has been studied in depth over a period of seventy-five years. The data in this archive include examples, illustrations, and raw materials for the study of almost all themes and issues relevant to the methodology of the social sciences, theories of the American community, and the study of American society. Muncie is the mother of "the science of Muncieology."

Back to Middletown is different in kind from the other Muncieological investigations. Professor Rita Caccamo, an Italian sociologist from Rome, examines the Middletown saga through the distinctive anthropological lens possessed by those who are not participants in the culture they study. In her examination of the studies and restudies of Muncie, she gives us, for the first time, a view of this American phenomenon from the perspective of an "other."

What circumstances prompted Professor Caccamo to abandon Rome for Muncie, Indiana? While a student in Rome, she had read *Middletown* and *Middletown in Transition,* published in translation in Italy in 1970, some forty years after the English editions appeared. In 1988, she met Whitney Gordon and Joseph Tamney—sociologists at Ball State University and caretakers of the Middletown legacy—who invited her to visit Muncie. Accepting the invitation in 1989, she used her own resources to make a short field trip reconnoitering the Muncie milieu and renewing her acquaintance with the Ball State sociologists. During this visit, Gordon and Tamney convinced Professor Caccamo to do an independent study of the contents of the Muncieological data bank.

For more than a year from 1989 through 1990, Caccamo researched the archives and lived in Muncie, observing it and experiencing the contemporary ethnographic reality of the town. This was her baptism into the way of life of the middle-sized Hoosier city she previously had encountered through the Lynds' books. Like the perspective of an anthropologist who restudies a tribe investigated by ethnographic predecessors, her perceptual angle of refraction was guided by both the earlier studies and her own current observations. She examined American culture, not as an emissary of a primitive tribe, but as an Italian academic whose cultural milieu has an historic depth exceeding that of Muncie, a cosmopolitan European, come to search and research the Muncian tribe and its sociological investigators.

It is ironic that *Back to Middletown* has the quality of an anthropological report—a quality the Lynds had originally hoped that their study would have. Conducting their research in the then uncharted territory of community studies, the Lynds sought the advice of the anthropologist Clark Wissler, who advised them to classify their observational data according to the prevailing canon of anthropological fieldwork. As Caccamo notes, this led the Lynds to make the following assumptions: "All the things people do in this American city may be viewed as falling under one or another of [Wissler's] six main-trunk activities: Getting a living; Making a home; Training the young; Using leisure in various forms of play, art, and so on; Engaging in religious practices; Engaging in community activities" (*RTM,* Chapter 2).

The Lynds gathered data under each of these categories but failed to assume an anthropological attitude, perhaps because they were participants in the culture they sought to examine. They shared with their informants

the American language and a Protestant religious orientation then dominant in Muncie. Moreover, Robert Lynd had spent the early years of his
life in Indiana. An anthropological perspective requires a sharp contrast
between the culture of the ethnographer and the culture of the native, en-
abling the ethnographer to "see" what the natives, embedded in their own
practices, cannot. It is only now, under Professor Caccamo's gaze, that
Muncie and the field of Muncieology are examined from the perspective
of norms that are not indigenous to them.

The original Middletown study was guided by worries about changes
in American values brought on by industrialization, urbanization, and
consumption. Postulating that these changes would have a negative effect
on traditional American values, the Lynds searched for a community that
had not yet been transformed by these changes. In Helen Lynd's words,
"Bob visited various cities, and decided that he didn't want a city with
large foreign population or a racially-mixed city."[1] Muncie was chosen as
a research site because it was thought to be less affected by modern trends.
It was also composed of, in Robert Lynd's words, good old "stock" that
still carried the older values of an integrated Protestant community—
hard-working, church-going, covenanted, and civic-minded citizens. The
Lynds "were convinced that the hope for social progress and moral
reawakening resided . . . within the original American spirit, the adventurous, strong spirit of the Protestant pioneers of the Midwest" (*RTM*,
Chapter 1). Lynd, himself a Protestant minister, hoped to preserve the
moral ethos of Protestantism and bring the gospel into the world by addressing pressing social problems. Sponsored by the Institute for Social
and Religious Research, a John D. Rockefeller philanthropy concerned
with the preservation of Christian values, his study was intended to assess
the state of traditional American values, to discover how they were changing, and to estimate the consequences. For this reason, Lynd chose not to
study a multiethnic city, as the Institute had proposed, but instead selected
"the traditional vanishing white, Anglo-Saxon, Protestant city, which was
for him the center of old-fashioned American virtue" (*RTM*, Chapter 1).
However, the Lynds found that the older values had already been deeply
eroded, even in Muncie. This major research finding was so troubling to
the Institute that it dissociated itself from the publication of *Middletown*.

The Lynds' focus on Muncie's changing values gave them their theoretical perspective and guided their substantive observations, determining
what they saw and how they saw it: the power and consistency of the
Middletown study can be attributed to the clarity of their research focus.
The Lynds discovered the dominance of consumer values over the older
Puritan virtues of frugality, austerity, and civic-mindedness, and learned
that the members of the community were no longer each other's moral

keepers. They also discovered that the moral standards of community members, which had once been determined by a faith in the moral equality of the faithful, had been replaced by competitive individualism and pecuniary standards of civic worth. Caccamo notes that Lynd had been influenced by Thorstein Veblen's book, *The Theory of the Leisure Class*, in which pecuniary values as standards of civic honor and status were first analyzed. Muncie's community covenant was sundered and replaced by a class system that divided the community between the "business class" and the "working class." Within the framework of their own moral values, the Lynds documented a major change in the character structure of middle America just as Veblen had done for the new American industrial aristocracy. Theirs was the first sociological study to portend the eclipse of the older dominant values of white, Anglo-Saxon, Protestant culture: the Puritan spirit had been defeated by the ethics of the modern corporation, new forms of industrial wealth, the emergence of a class system, and the failure of civic and religious leaders to uphold the covenant. These findings are the reason *Middletown* is still in print and worth reading today.

However, the Lynds' focus on changes in the older values obscured other, more salient trends that were crucial to Muncie's development. As Professor Caccamo notes, the Lynds' decision not to study an ethnically mixed community led them to ignore Muncie's religious minorities, its "hillbillies" and Negroes, as they were then known. These groups had already appeared in the Middletown of the 1920's and were not easily accommodated by the norms of the dominant white, Anglo-Saxon, Protestant majority. Their values penetrated deeply into the life of the community and were influential in the development of ethnic particularism and nationalism. The Lynds failed to observe that these "foreigners" in their midst would supply Muncie with new values. These newer lifestyles were not based on un-American ideas, but rather have emerged from fundamental organizational, economic, educational, and demographic changes not only in Muncie but the rest of the country as well.

Changes in the educational needs of business and industry, not noted by the Lynds, had appeared in Muncie in the 1920's. In 1918, Muncie's leading family had arranged for the purchase of the property of the old Eastern Indiana Normal School. In collaboration with the State Board of Education, it became a teachers college and later, under the aegis of the state of Indiana, was transformed into Ball State University. This university now has a student body of twenty thousand in a city with a population of eighty thousand. These demographics may be taken as a measure of the shift from the older religious promises of salvation to the university as the community's pivotal agency of secular salvation. Although they witnessed, recorded, and lamented the decline of Protestant values, the Lynds did not grasp the subtleties of the transvaluations of those values in the emerging secular culture.

Numerous commentators have criticized the Middletown study for its failure to so much as mention Muncie's dominant industrial family, the Ball brothers, and their philanthropical endeavors. This lapse was not an oversight, but was rather due to the Lynds' commitment to the civic values of the Ball family: "Early on we were invited to dinner, first by Mrs. Stevens, who was a social leader, and then by the Balls."[2] From the point of view of Protestant theology, the Ball brothers were stewards of their worldly wealth, a divinely imposed moral obligation for those who enjoy economic success and bear a special responsibility to the community. In their philanthropic activities, the Ball brothers were not only instrumental in creating the teachers college and developing it into Ball State University, but over the years they also gave money to Muncie's churches, the hospital, the YMCA, and a library, as well as other philanthropic enterprises in many other parts of the country. The Lynds' failure to mention the Ball brothers in their first volume suggests that they regarded the presence of an overwhelmingly dominant family in Muncie as the norm, not worthy of special notice. Because of his own Protestant ethos Lynd did not see a central institutional feature of the American community.

There is a twofold irony to this story. First, the Ball brothers were acting out a pattern of stewardship in Muncie, just as the Rockefellers, who sponsored the Lynds, were acting out a similar pattern in New York and in the country as a whole. Divine stewardship in this world meant improving life on earth through the good works of educational uplift, technological advance, and the improvement of health and welfare, a project to which Lynd as a clergyman gave his implicit assent. He was appalled, however, by the Rockefellers' treatment of workers at the Elk Basin oil camp, which Lynd had visited and, to the annoyance of John D. Rockefeller, had published his findings in the article "Done in Oil," a muckraking attack on big-business labor policies. Committed to the values of the social gospel, Lynd did not see the connection between his own gospel values and the values of Protestantism when expressed in the economic ethic of capitalism. Second, and more important, Lynd's ideological commitment prevented him not only from seeing a central fact of the social structure of the community, but from generalizing it into a common institutional pattern in the United States. American communities have typically been built up around a major industry dominated by a few families. In the past, the wealth of leading families, including that of the Ball brothers, was used circumspectly and without ostentation, directed to philanthropic goals rather than the direct purchase of political favors, honorifics, and influence, as has come to be the contemporary norm. The Ball brothers' philanthropic reinvestments in the community made them socially dominant and politically influential outside the framework of political institutions, meaning that politicians listened to their opinions and anticipated their reactions before acting on controversial local issues that touched on the Balls' jurisdictional interests in social and economic matters. In our book *Small Town in Mass Society*, Joseph Bensman and I referred to this phenomenon as an "invisible government": its existence still remains as one of the great secrets about how American democracy functions at all local, state, and national levels. At the time of the first Middletown study, Lynd accepted these arrangements as unremarkable axioms of leadership and political power in American life.

Much was to change in both Lynd and Middletown as a result of the financial and industrial depression of the decade of the thirties and its aftermath, the post–World War II golden age of American capitalism. After encountering the writing of Marx, Lynd became sympathetic to the communist experiment in the Soviet Union and a critic of American politics and economy, which he saw as the perversion of the social gospel by capitalism. This change in attitude was reproduced in many other Protestant ministers and sociologists, including Albion Small at the University of Chicago, who had hoped to transform Marxism into a form of Christian socialism. The Lynds' restudy of Muncie, *Middletown in Transition: A Study in Cultural Conflicts*, rests on a different set of premises. These new research premises led Lynd to analyze the social position of the Ball brothers in a chapter of the book devoted to "The X Family," which he described as a "reigning royal family" exemplifying "a pattern of business class control." The change in Lynd's values demonstrates the relationship between an investigator's values and his or her findings with a clarity not generally found in sociological studies.

In Chapters 4 and 5, Rita Caccamo addresses some controversial ethical and methodological issues uncovered by her searches of the Muncieological data bank. She explains: "When we sociologists go to 'look,' we find not only treasures, but also rubbish, black holes, points of no return. . . . Like a deep-sea diver I had to decide whether to leave what I had found where it lay or to bring it to the surface." To let it lie, she says, "might have been a useless act of piety." Her soul-searching refers to her discovery of a study of Middletown written as a dissertation in history at the University of Colorado by Lynn Perrigo, who had been a teacher in Middletown at the time of the Lynds' first study, and whose conception of Middletown differed from that of the Lynds.

In his dissertation, Perrigo faults the Lynds' first study for failing to mention the social and economic importance of the Ball brothers. During their restudy, the Lynds had access to Perrigo's work, which is reflected in their chapter on the X family in *Middletown in Transition*. Perrigo's work is cited as a "local source," an attribution to which he never objected: it was a source, however, which supported the Lynds' new values. Only later, when Middletown was restudied in the 1970's by Caplow's research team, in the project called Middletown III, did the Perrigo case become an issue. Howard Bahr, a field director for this later study, wrote an essay published in the *Indiana Magazine of History*, in which, Caccamo notes, he "sets up a sort of trial of the Lynds, without ever accusing them directly of plagiarism, but rather of a somewhat cavalier use of the information furnished by Perrigo." Apparently, Bahr had originally submitted this essay to Edward Lauman, then the editor of the *American Journal of Sociology*, who solicited the advice of Robert K. Merton concerning its publication. The story of Lauman's diplomatic solicitation of Lynd's Columbia colleague, Merton, whose statesmanlike intervention in the case led Bahr to publish his essay elsewhere, is told delicately and subtly by Caccamo. The reader of Chapter 4 will find enlightening the in-house resolution of this problem by the sociological establishment.

Middletown III, evaluated by Caccamo in Chapter 5, was directed by Professor Theodore Caplow of the University of Virginia, who had been a student of Lynd at Columbia University. Although his project was supported with a large grant from the National Science Foundation, and was carried out with a staff of researchers and their administrative assistants, only two of its six projected volumes have been published. It employed the modus operandi of social survey research, thus inviting a comparison with the two-person participant observation method employed by the Lynds. Caccamo's comparison of the methods and substantive findings of the three Middletown studies bears on such fundamental issues as (1) the limitations produced by the ahistoricity of survey research: Middletown III tells us nothing of the many Munciean changes that had taken place in the intervening fifty years; (2) the inappropriateness of the method of replication—drawn from the experimental sciences in social investigations—of the Lynds' survey categories by the Middletown III researchers; and (3) the place of a disciplined personal vision to give artistic expression to prevailing social realities. This reader is left with the impression that Professor Caplow thought he was doing a form of social science that would discredit and eliminate the role of the person in social research; in fact, his methodological approach was responsible for the failure of his project.

The Ball brothers no longer have an industrial presence in Muncie. By the 1960's, the glass canning jars on which their original wealth was based were manufactured elsewhere. With the development of new technologies related to the manufacture of glass, they engaged in a variety of related industries: packaging (glass containers, metal closures, home canning supplies, and plastic containers); graphic arts (photoengraving plates and chemicals, zinc lithographer's plates, and lithographed and coated metals); industrial specialties (zinc battery cans, molded and extruded rubber and plastic parts, gaskets, decorative plastics); aerospace manufacturing; and electronics. As Donald Birt wrote in 1969, in a paper submitted to me in a course on the American community, all these specialties grew out of the original problem of how to make a canning jar (rubber- and zinc-coated lids) for home purposes. During the Cold War, the Ball enterprises were recipients of governmental contracts for the production of ceramics needed for satellites and America's space program. Becoming both a national and international enterprise, the Balls moved their headquarters elsewhere and removed themselves from the arena of local and state politics, raising their political status to a national level and addressing their philanthropic endeavors to those communities in which the labor force worked in their factories. The descendants of the Ball brothers became members of interlocking banking, transportation, industrial, church, and political party directorates on which they can claim a voice in making national and international policy.

The story of the Ball brothers is, in microcosm, a history of the changing social, political, and economic roles of America's dominant industrial families. It is also the story of what happened to American small towns and cities when their original primary industrial base collapsed. The Muncieological data bank contains plenty of gold for social scientific prospectors who wish to understand the histories of American communities and their leading families. *Back to Middletown* joins *Middletown* and *Middletown in Transition* as another benchmark study in the saga of American social, economic, and political history.

Preface to the American Edition

THE ROADS ARE FEW that lead to Muncie, Indiana, the city that the Lynds made famous during the twenties and thirties as "Middletown," a prototype of industrial white, Anglo-Saxon, Protestant America. As Helen Lynd would note in her posthumously published memoirs, *Possibilities* (1983), Muncie was chosen "precisely because there was nothing exceptional about it"; like other American Middletowns, it was "typical"—historically, sociologically, and geographically average.

The city is hardly a sought-after destination for tourists looking for postcard vistas and spectacular, exotic sites. On the contrary, the great midwestern prairies around Muncie/Middletown, with their immense spaces, strong winds, and sparse human population, tend to bewilder the European who visits them for the first time.

The town now extends to include suburbs and shopping malls. At first, the older neighborhoods, with their broad lawns and tall trees—the area around the university campus, for example—seem like pleasant places to live, especially during the day. People look nice and seem kind. Later, however, the visitor from abroad comes to have a very different impression: he or she begins to experience the anonymity and isolation that are typical of more metropolitan areas. The sense of being in a community, in a neighborhood where people know and care about each other, is supplanted by a feeling of alienation—of being in a strange, unfamiliar place.

The Lynds' research on Middletown is one of the most famous community studies in the history of sociology. Other well-known investigations that focus on the problem of community within large cities include William White's *Street Corner Society* and Gerald Suttles's *The Social Order of the Slum*. These in turn are aligned with earlier thinking—including that of Robert Park and Ernest Burgess of the University of Chicago Department of Sociology—on the "natural community" that takes shape within a seemingly impersonal and anonymous large city (Suttles 1972). Descriptive studies that emphasize fieldwork and examine social structure as a spatial phenomenon are the hallmark of the highly influential Chicago School of sociology, which formed and flourished during the twenties and thirties.

It is not only difficult to describe a community experientially; it is controversial, even among contemporary social researchers. First of all, it is problematic to define the distinguishing characteristics of community: that on which its experience and integration are based; its unique functions and tasks; the social units within it and the interactions among these units; the economic and social bases of the community structure; the relationship and distinction between internal social structure and macrosocial structures external to the community; the relationship between personal experience and behavior, and communal experience and behavior; the causes and processes of transformation from *Gemeinschaft* to *Gesellschaft* states of social existence; and community continuity and adaptation in the face of social change.

Although certain observations about the nature of human societies, the disruption of communal structures, and the rise of formal, impersonal social institutions are difficult to reject, explanations of the decline of community generally offer an either-or proposition: either communal structure has "limited liability," or the process from "community" to "society" is not a linear and continuous one. As Edgar F. Borgatta points out:

According to the community of limited liability thesis, networks of human association and interdependence are argued to exist at various levels of social organization, and social status characteristics are identified that are associated with differentiated levels of participation in community life, e.g., the family life cycle phase. The idea of "limited liability" poses the argument that, in a highly mobile society, the attachments to community tend to be based on rationalism rather than on sentiment and that even those "invested" in the community are limited in their sense of personal commitment. (Borgatta and Borgatta 1992)

Fieldwork seems to show that in metropolitan areas it is possible to reproduce community only in terms of "limited liability." In his study of suburban Levittown, New Jersey, in the late sixties, Herbert Gans stressed the new forms of decision making in the local community. In his words, the research is

not a defense of suburbia, but a study of a single new suburb, Levittown, N.J., in which I lived as a "participant observer" for the first two years of its existence to find out how a new community comes into being, how people change when they leave the city, and how they live and politic in suburbia. Nor is it a defense of sociology, but an application of my own conception of it and its methods. (Gans 1967)

As the Lynds emphasize in their depiction of Middletown, community spirit was increasingly giving way to the ideology of consumerism and the accumulation of wealth. The Middletown citizen of the twenties and thirties, as described by Lynd and by the city's inhabitants themselves, gave a false impression of being happy in his or her comfortable conformity, which, although not apparently detrimental, ultimately impoverished his or her identity and ability to change. The Lynds foresaw that the transformation Muncie/Middletown was undergoing would eventually affect the whole of American society.

The two young researchers Robert and Helen Lynd intended to study social change in the relatively homogeneous and uniform provinces of the Midwest. When they began their research on Muncie, the strong sense of group solidarity in frontier communities was very much in decline. As the century waned, American historians recognized the end of the period of the pioneers (Turner [1920] 1976). It is no coincidence that the Lynds took as their fixed point of reference the year 1890 in their description of the contemporary changes occurring in Middletown, the average small American city. The midwestern America they were studying in the twenties was very different from that of only thirty years earlier. The Lynds' work was situated in the midst of this epoch-making transition, and they intended their writing to identify and reflect on the multicultural American phenomena taking place in Middletown society.

The sociologist observing America in the twenties recognized that cultural patterns in America were shifting. Stable settlements, the expansion of urban centers and cities, massive industrialization, mass immigration and its resulting ethnic problems, and the organization of work on a vast scale—all had completely changed the American social scene, and all were studied by sociologists in terms of the specific forms they assumed and their consequences. Literary writers and social scientists—economists, historians, and sociologists—were reexamining the frontier hypothesis. Even today, sociologists are inquiring into the Lynds' statements about frontier-induced mobility and Americans on the move—like hoboes and other migrants—as products of the pioneering heritage.

The Lynds discovered that the new values emerging in America were materialistic and self-centered rather than symbolic and altruistic (Riesman 1950). In their view, the small city represented the place where the traditional "good" values of the American pioneers (the white, Anglo-Saxon, Protestant spirit) were crushed by industrialization and the resulting class divisions (working class and business class). In addition, the "American dream" of upward mobility, typical of the American colonial pioneering spirit, was disappearing. As Alexis de Tocqueville had feared many years earlier, the frontier spirit had become a mere appropriation that, deprived of the spirit of community, no longer offered any guarantee of "democracy."

For a European scholar, the decade from 1920 to 1930 in the United States represented a critical point both for the development of the "new" science of sociology and for the late-modern social scenario. In Europe at the time, sociology had not yet been established as an officially recognized, empirical discipline (Caccamo 1997). Meanwhile, Chicago sociologists such as Thomas and Park believed the tendency toward heterogeneity in the great metropolis was indicative of nationwide changes. Hinterland versus metropolis, homogeneity versus heterogeneity, radical criticism versus reformism: the Lynds and the Chicagoans united in their efforts to redirect the changes that were shaking American society. Chicago became both the real and the symbolic place of the increasing "diversity"; numerous studies were done on ethnicity and other deviances from the old norms.

While the Lynds' approach was to focus on "normality," the Chicagoans chose to study instances of deviance. The first was based on a desire to radically transform apparently tranquil normality; the second aimed to reshape diversity into normality via a vast program of social reform. Both believed that sociology was the most efficacious instrument for understanding the observed world and transforming it.

The Chicago scholars' approach to sociology was more "scientific" than the Lynds': the Chicagoans not only adhered to a precisely defined discipline, study methods, and interrelated "objects" of study; they also sought to establish and found the institutionalization of sociology as a science officially recognized for its methods, prospectives, and schools.

The differences between the Lynds' approach and that of the Chicago "sociologists in action" were at times difficult to discern but were nonetheless marked, in that the Lynds believed America had to be completely rebuilt while the Chicago scholars favored a systematic social plan within existing conditions (Vidich and Lyman 1985). It is no coincidence that Robert Lynd first studied theology in Manhattan and obtained a bachelor's degree in divinity; his doctorate in sociology followed many years afterward. Even the journalist-sociologist Robert Park in his biography of Lynd observed that Lynd's sociological research was infused with the spirit of an "ethical mission," and that Lynd viewed his research as a place where the complicated dynamics of disintegration and reintegration were enacted.

The Chicago School of sociology was trying to deal with the problems emerging in American society from another viewpoint, one that perceived the metropolis as a social laboratory for change at every level. The Chicagoans were trying to comprehend how a "limited liability" community could be reproduced in metropolitan areas. The Lynds, however, were trying to understand the process of disintegration in an old community. While research on big cities such as Chicago has shown that the direction of social change in America of the twenties was extremely discontinuous and varied in its forms and expressions, investigation of Middletown revealed the decidedly negative character of change in terms of social structure and cultural values. Those positive elements that could be recovered in the imperfect melting pot of the metropolis were discovered to be completely lost and beyond recovery in the scenario outlined by the Lynds. Real improvement in the conditions of the material and symbolic life of the citizens did not seem possible in Muncie/Middletown: blocked economic mobility and consumerism characterized that context. On the other hand, the reformers of the Chicago School were able to glimpse the possibility of a better world in which conflict would be reduced and social change would enable progress toward a better society. The historical confrontation between the liberal Chicagoans and the radical Lynds showed a common area of involvement but a clear, basic difference in approach or, in Mannheim's terms, in ideology.

Further research into the effects of globalization on community identity could turn out to be extremely useful for distinguishing contemporary transformations in Muncie, Indiana, although today's more relevant sociological approach makes it difficult to agree with the Lynds' interpretation in certain critical areas. Firstly, their working-class-versus-business-class view of socioeconomic division appears to be an overly simple interpretation of the complex dynamics of social groupings and the role of the individual in American society, not only at the end of the millennium but also at the time of the Lynds' first study. In the twenties, social change in both large and small towns was multiple, not just polarized into that of two opposite social groups. The Lynds' critique of American social structure was limited in that it obscured instances of deviation from conformity; immigrants, newcomers, and outsiders were not presented as an important part of the American scenario. The Lynds did not seem to see the complex dialectic among social change, deviance, integration, and conflict. Also problematic is the fact that the Lynds' conception of power was based on their theory of social stratification. As Polsby proposes in his book on community power, studies on social stratification make five assertions about power in American communities:

1. The upper class rules in local community life.
2. Political and civic leaders are subordinate to the upper class.
3. A single "power elite" rules in the community.
4. The upper-class power elite rules in its own interests.
5. Social conflict takes place between the upper and lower classes.

Polsby underlines the recurrent risk of ideological bias in social-stratification theory. Referring to the Lynds' approach he states,

This oldest of the stratification studies of community life is in many ways the best, since all five generalizations which seem to characterize stratification analyses of community power are set forth and accompanied by a wealth of circumstantial detail. Indeed, one of the Lynds' greatest contributions is the care and responsibility with which they recorded data that disproves the proposition of stratification theory, in spite of the fact that they themselves adhere to these propositions. This is, of course, the ultimate tribute to their skill as reporters. (Polsby 1980)

The Lynds' perspective tended to view modernity as linked exclusively to the industrialization process that produced consumerism as a way of life. In the last decade, many scholars in the field of sociology have studied the phenomena and features of late modern society—its limitations and its resources. Modernizing processes continuously develop new meanings in addition to the ideologies of the accumulation of wealth and consumerism: world-wide mobility, socialization over distance, but also new doubts and insecurities. However, as a complex social process, modernity does not imply only the loss of certainty, but also encourages people to be more adventurous and to experience new lifestyles—to build new lives. Risk and trust are two sides of the same coin. As Ulrich Beck points out about the process of modernity:

There is, of course, an ongoing history of loss and destruction, but there is also an irreversible acceptance of modernity which is often even a precondition for its critique. . . . Behind the image of rootlessness hides a flaw in reasoning. We try to shut our own consent to modernity so as not to lose the yardstick of critique which is posited more and more or above all in that which is past and in that which is lost. An important test of modernity's capacity for self-criticism is its way of dealing systematically with self-inflicted basic errors: how secure is that "ontological" security in the face of the potential for destruction which industrialism has by now universalized by turning it into a good media story and making it comprehensible? (Beck 1992)

This crucial question remains unanswered since everything is open and ambivalent—and risky—in modern society, and these important features of modernity stay completely in the background of the Lynds' critique of American society of their time. They thought that only a noncapitalistic society could restore a system of values and solidarity, and that America had to be "remade from the foundations."

Their sociological imagination was not varied enough to be able to glimpse other solutions to or outcomes of industrial capitalist systems. In later phases of modernity, new forms of solidarity and trust seem to have been produced, even beyond face-to-face relationships. In Giddens's terms, larger and larger areas of social life are removed from the here and now, stretching away in time and space: in late modernity, people do not have to be physically present to each other in order to interact or to re-create living forms of community (Giddens 1990). The Lynds' disquisition on the consequences of industrial capitalist systems is an endless work of reflection on systems, institutions, and social protagonists.

The Lynds also feared the effects on community of an economic development that has so extended today's global dimension as to be considered the end of community. In contemporary sociology, this subject is once again becoming central to inquiry into the ambivalence associated with globalizing processes, global culture, and the intrinsic distinction between distance and proximity, integration and disintegration, assimilation and difference.

The present book begins with a portrait of the career of Robert S. Lynd, continues with an examination of the class divisions in Middletown in the twenties and of the collapse of the town's social structure and sense of community in the wake of modernization, and completes its examination of the Lynds' studies with a look at Middletown's demise after the Depression—the town's crumbling social foundations and loss of "spirit."

In the Lynds' second study, they claimed to perceive an overwhelming elitism in Middletown that completely controlled all the lower socioeconomic groups during this time of transition. Manipulation was a one-way process; there was no chance for the poorer or even the average American to construct—in keeping with the American dream—his or her own social destiny. In connection with this second study, *Middletown in Transition*, the present book reviews the debate over the sources used by the Lynds to increase their understanding of the role of the powerful "X family." Chapter 4 is dedicated to examining the effect of Lynn Perrigo—a scholar and a native of Middletown whose insights about this matter influenced the Lynds—as an anonymous source for this study.

Return to Middletown ends with a brief consideration of the interpretations of the 1970's and 1980's relative to the issue of whether or not Muncie/Middletown will be able to survive within a global society. I hope that this book will help the reader think about Middletown's prospects in the context of present changes.

Rita Caccamo

Back to Middletown

Robert S. Lynd: Portrait of an Author

Social Science and Ethical Mission

A biographer often has difficulty identifying the circumstances, events, and people that have most influenced an individual's life. A biographical study reveals recurring elements and underlying links in a life that from time to time disappear, only to reappear suddenly in a different form, or even to dissolve altogether.[1] This discontinuity—both in the direction of the investigation and in the interests and creative output of the subject—is a persistent problem that cannot be resolved simply by analyzing a "career" or an official curriculum vitae. The problem is better explored "by descending the mine shaft," groping underground for the hidden thread that led the person along through various intellectual diversions, before finally guiding him up to the light (Devereux 1980; Anzieu 1981).

Venturing is the word Robert Staughton Lynd used to describe his intellectual development from his youth onward. As a young man, uncertain of the future but animated by a profound sense of social calling, Lynd enrolled in 1920 at Union Theological Seminary in Manhattan, a Presbyterian institution. The force of that calling would first bring him success but later condemn him to silence.

His undying radicalism could be recognized even in the first papers he wrote while pursuing his bachelor of divinity—a radicalism that would eventually break him during his difficult confrontations with the sociological and political ideas that would gain the upper hand in America after the Second World War.

In one of his papers he wrote for his B.D., entitled *Has Preaching a Function in Adult Re-education?* and published in 1921, the young Robert identified two categories of Christian preacher: traditional and experimental. The traditional preacher preferred to run the risk of believing too much and being wrong, rather than believing too little, while the experimental preacher challenged orthodoxy. Preaching served an important social and socializing function, but its means and its ends could vary from extreme dogmatism to subversion. As Lynd had already argued in an earlier paper, *A Critique of Preaching from the Standpoint of Modern Educational Method*, insofar as it was "teaching from the pulpit," preaching could be the mere "delivery of a self-atoning monologue," whereas it should be a means for the reeducation of adults. Such preaching, however, runs the risk of provoking serious damage. Unlike old-fashioned exhortation, but like inductive scientific procedures, the modern sermon undertakes psychological and moral education through feeling, by rousing emotions and then ordering them according to meaning.

The alternative to the traditional preacher was the experimental preacher who, in the spirit of Dewey, accepted the responsibilities of contemporary life and attempted to communicate their uncertainties and consequences. The conventional figure of the preacher working within a dogmatic system had become obsolete, and Lynd saw the "free" lecturer as more useful, whether in the classroom, in public debate, or in informal discussion. Lynd concluded that people should be encouraged to look for religion not in churches among preachers, in agencies, or in official bodies, but in their everyday activities with their fellow human beings.

It was precisely the ritualization of religion, however, its formalism and the resulting loss of deep religious meaning, that Lynd and his wife, Helen, would find in "Middletown." But the two young researchers realized that other social phenomena were linked to the process of secularization, and they did not want to ignore these. The original objective of their study was thus destined to change, in the spirit of "discovery," and the entire urban landscape would provide the background for their narrative about one cross-section of America in the 1930's. Not by chance, the first volume on Middletown would be subtitled *A Study in Modern American Culture* (1929). The Lynds' intellectual and lay adventure had begun.

The coincidence of internal demands and external conditions gave young Lynd the opportunity of practicing his beliefs without "betraying" his religious education. He accepted the opportunity of working on the "Small City Study" project offered to him by John Rockefeller's Institute of Social and Religious Research (ISRR). After his experience of preaching and social activism at Elk Basin (an oil camp in Wyoming) during the summer of 1922,[2] Lynd seemed to his scientific sponsors to be the ideal man for delicate research into the "new" social restlessness and the ensuing transformation of "good" old-fashioned American values. However, the observatory would no longer be a desolate, isolated village populated by people who were exhausted by hard work and exploitation, but a tranquil, "average" American city. This was how the idea of the "Small City Study" came about. The goal of the analysis, then, was not academic, but was meant to include social and religious interests, using the methods of social science, in order to renew the American social and moral order. Sociology would knit together the tearings in the social fabric as traditional religious faith was superseded by ethical mission.

In his lectures, Lynd had already denounced the figure of the preacher and the usefulness of preaching, and his antidogmatic spirit prevented him from continuing his studies at Union Theological Seminary. He found in the lessons of Dewey his basic, lasting orientation to scientific research; Dewey's convictions—about the value of freely adopted, different points of view, for example—held for Robert the character of a revelation. At thirty years of age, he had finally grasped the "relativity" of knowledge and the "eclectic," pragmatic approach.

With this new understanding, it was clear that he could no longer preach. Preaching meant manipulating the conscience, and he wanted to discover a vast social world. Fears began to surface, however: the fear—which he described later in *Knowledge for What?* (1939)—of drowning in an infinity of facts and correlations. Though galvanized by the discovery of the experimental method, he had already glimpsed how an empiricism separate from practical issues would eventually freeze the will to act. Lynd's transformation into a sociologist, a scholar detached from society, became a means of distancing himself from the temptation of imposing his values on human beings, a temptation to which he had fallen prey at the Wyoming oil camp. As shown by the papers written for his B.D., Lynd's research in Middletown fulfilled his undisclosed goal of helping people face their problems actively without resorting to solutions prefabricated by others. Investigation into Muncie's problems would force Lynd to search continuously for the right balance between scientific and ethical demands.

The new ideology of consumption combined religious and secular motivations (Campbell 1987), and those who analyzed the new consumer society appealed to religious as well as to lay norms and values. Lynd decided to introduce into *Middletown* the problem of the moral legitimacy of the emerging orientation toward consumerism in America. Only after three years of conflict and debate in the ISRR was Lynd able to formulate a viewpoint that linked moral criticism to scientific analysis; it was that particular perspective that gave *Middletown* its originality and its strength. In a reminiscence of 1924, Lynd declared that his objective was "to define and measure the changes in the life, in the habits and behavior, of a little city because such changes have important effects on religious problems."[3]

The true intention of the two young researchers, the Lynds, went beyond that diplomatic declaration: namely, to follow their own inclinations and to convince their sponsors of the validity of their research and conclusions. Over and beyond the facts, it would be necessary to investigate values and to develop criticism to focus on them.

The "Average" City and Its Values

Lynd and his wife, Helen, who worked alongside him, especially in his first research,[4] chose the "homogeneous" Muncie because they were convinced that the hope for social progress and moral reawakening resided wholly within the original American spirit, the adventurous, strong spirit of the Protestant pioneers of the Midwest. Muncie offered the stage for the unfolding drama of capitalistic consumption, which was starting to filter into the lives of those honest, hard-working people who perhaps still had a chance of defending themselves against the easy temptations of consumerism, to orient their destiny in an independent direction.

Lynd refused the project for the study of an ethnically divided city, proposed at the time by the Institute, and thus refused as well the research model implicit to it. The Chicago School, and Robert Park in particular, held that the "mixed," heterogeneous city best represented modern society. Lynd chose instead the traditional, vanishing white, Anglo-Saxon, Protestant city, which was for him the symbolic center of old-fashioned American virtue (Curti 1950). Thus two different concepts of "typicalness" in the urban context—homogeneity versus heterogeneity—were compared, with an eye on the contrasting social phenomena. In spring 1926, as work progressed and chapters were completed, the financing institute became aware that the initial "spiritual" objective had been substituted with Lynd's "universal cultural approach." This new anthropological perspective modified the researcher's attitude toward the subject of his study, introducing into it ever more critical detachment and irony.

Following in the footsteps of Veblen (author of *The Theory of Leisure Class* [1899]), Robert, a native of Indiana returning home after a long absence, assumed the attitude of the naive observer coming to Muncie the way Margaret Mead disembarked in Samoa. This change in strategy was made possible also by the benevolence of Clark Wissler, who was at that time the director of the Museum of Natural History in New York City. The well-known Wissler—who wrote a brief preface to the first volume on Middletown—was, for Lynd, a double resource: a highly respected social scientist who had grown up in the Midwest only thirty-five miles from Muncie. He thus had direct knowledge of the city and could endorse the scientific objectivity of Lynd's work.

In reality, this was the first research by an American sociologist that referred to the concept of culture in its entirety along the line already indicated by Malinowsky and Radcliffe-Brown. With *Middletown*, the Lynds described a cultural system in which every aspect of life functioned as part of a whole, though not without tensions and inconsistencies within. The couple singled out the "money culture" as the pivot around which the individual and collective existence of Muncie's local population turned; the pecuniary culture that Veblen had noticed thirty years earlier in the dominant class had by now been extended to the whole of society. With this as their frame of reference, the Lynds may have exaggerated the uniformity of Muncie in the years between 1890 and 1924 so as to be able to affirm that sociologically, morally, and politically Americans were on the verge of abandoning their democratic and cultural heritage. According to this view, the hypothesis that Americans were adhering more and more to the emerging ideologies of money and consumerism could be demonstrated through empirical investigation. The Lynds therefore chose to compare two times and two worlds, 1890 and 1924; in the latter, Muncie was disoriented, already in transition between two different systems of cultural values. When the Lynds came to study Middletown during the 1920's they found that the old values had been substituted with new ones; individualism had taken the place of heredity; the pursuit of money, success, and consumption had become the central values. With the advent of a "pecuniary age" (Dewey 1929), the supremacy of money had come to be contrasted with the work ethic.

The choice of Muncie became an ever clearer interpretative advantage: unlike the big city riven by ethnic and racial conflicts, fragmented and anonymous, conflict was easily identified in Middletown at both a personal and collective level. While the Lynds maintained the concept of the active individual, Park, the founding father of the Chicago School of sociology, believed that urbanization was an impersonal process in which the individual had no determining role: individuals were fish caught in the river of social change. Park believed that the typical modern person was a being who was acted upon, not one who acted: he or she was an outsider, a member of the crowd, a deviant (1952). In their less deterministic approach, the Lynds extolled the individual's potential "resistance" to the process of becoming absorbed into the masses in which every capacity for recognizing the futility of consumer culture is crushed. During the course of their investigation, however, their initial optimism became obscured by the evidence. It had already become impossible to imagine a return to the 1890's, with its spontaneous leisure activities and forms of relaxation that were not subject to dominant fashions. There was a noticeable decline in family activities such as singing together, participating in choral groups, reading aloud, bicycling, going for country walks, going camping.

Research on big cities such as Chicago demonstrated that social change in America of the 1920's was extremely heterogeneous and various. Investigation into Middletown illustrated the decidedly negative character of the changes in terms of social structures and cultural values. Where the Chicago School predicted a better world in which conflict would be reduced and society would change for the better, the Lynds revealed that little was redeemable in the urban melting pot. There seemed to be no hope of real improvement in the lives of citizens in Muncie/Middletown, for whom blocked mobility and consumerism were the dominant realities.

The good customs of the past were disappearing and industrialization had undermined the very basis of society. Machine production had not only eliminated the distinction between unqualified and qualified labor (M. Stein 1960), but had also eliminated the apprentice system as a guarantee of vocational continuity within the same family. The home was no longer a center of economic production and social life, but only a point of departure for members of the family, each one of whom headed his or her own way to spend free time with his or her own group of friends. Unlike in 1890, when old-fashioned values were still intact, the citizens of Middletown in 1924 no longer gathered together to debate opinions, values, and individual or collective goals in the various public rooms of the city; nor did they hold meetings any longer to discuss philosophical, ethical, and political themes, let alone ideas of a more abstruse nature (Lynd and Lynd 1937). Moreover, although Middletown's residents no longer read serious books, low-grade fiction had a great following; newspapers had become the mouthpieces for advertising; public education, even at its most extensive, no longer had the goal of stimulating curiosity in young minds, but rather of instilling in them prefabricated values. Even religion, once spontaneous and permeating the life of the city, had lost its old power and had to resort to advertising to gain adherents.

These rapid changes had confused Muncie; the Lynds described the population as scrambling and competing for position along the social ladder. Everyone, both business people and working people, were frenetically involved in defending their accumulations of money, earned with more or less difficulty, to satisfy their growing needs. Massive advertising, together with magazines, films, radio, and so on, were rapidly changing life's priorities. Paradoxically, these insistent agents of change were welcomed by the consumers themselves. And all of this served to demonstrate the Lynds' theory about the increasing depersonalization of work and the consequent "decline of the community." Consumption compensated for the loss of the work ethic and the sense of community, the two cardinal elements in the social history of Middletown.

The Lynds made it clear that the social changes in Middletown had external roots and distant geographical origins. At the time of their observation, in fact, there were no noteworthy social conflicts in Muncie and, certainly, class struggle was not the origin of the changes. Workers, though organized, had lost their enthusiasm once their vocational skills had been eroded. In 1924, headlines in Muncie proposed the following prescriptions for local prosperity: "The duty of the citizen is to produce," and "The American is important to his country no longer as a citizen but as a consumer. Consumption is the new necessity." Individual Muncie citizens found themselves besieged, with their backs to the wall, in the face of such coercion, such brusque inversion of the values of work and savings that they had been taught for generations.

The "new" culture of consumption and hedonism represented a break with the past for both social classes studied by the Lynds, the business and the working class. While acquisitive capacity might differ for the two, the response by both was substantially similar. The Lynds' conviction that consumers were inspired and manipulated from outside demonized every form of human behavior in their eyes. They believed that the culture of consumption was dangerous because it fostered a view of human beings as consumers only, while in the areas of production and politics they no longer had an active role. This new reality pushed the single individual to acquire more than to create. Finally, because of their own "social ignorance," the massive attack from outside, and lack of self-perception, the inhabitants of Middletown were not prepared for consumption's onslaught and thus could not withstand it. With Dewey, the Lynds believed that human beings possessed the capacity to understand the "cultural configuration" of their time and could mobilize to defend their democratic base. In order to do this, they felt, it was necessary to put into action an efficient control plan that would stimulate individual growth and impede the hegemony of blind fortuitousness.

Like all social planners, the Lynds did not lack uncertainties that at times amounted to genuine contradictions. They yearned for a more methodical and organized social life, for more collective solidarity in Muncie and in all of America. At the same time, however, they welcomed "spontaneity," the unexpected, as a social virtue and they mistrusted certain new forms of false organization that the consumer culture imposed on free time, on diffusion of information, on religion, on politics—on every sphere of social life. Here, the two researchers reveal their own confusion and the difficulty of finding solutions. Which was more fearful: chance or method? spontaneity or organization?

At times, the Lynds seem to grope along in the cultural contradictions of their time, in the enormous, and perhaps pointless, effort of providing universal solutions that they often simply invented on the spot.[5] In his retirement, Robert Lynd believed that he had been unable to find replies to questions that were larger than himself, and that he had been opposed to reasonable, practicable, "middle-range" solutions (Merton 1949). In sociology, "middle-range theories" represent a dimension of analysis that moves away from speculative generalizations, unconcerned with theory. They are based on the relation between theory and research as a direct means of developing and establishing the validity of social theory. For Robert Lynd, the problems of the whole contrasted with specific problems in his sociological work, and the total commitment of his detached intellect was at odds with the mechanisms of politics.

Lynd Against the Consumer: Analysis and Action

The Lynds had encountered together the problems of consumption in Middletown. Robert Lynd committed himself to do more research on the subject, and took on a more active position when he began to collaborate with the economist Wesley Mitchell (1912) toward the Social Science Research Council in 1927. Lynd ran into certain objections, however, on the part of the senior and well-respected sociologist William Ogburn, the theorist of "cultural lag."[6] When Lynd became a part of the President's Research Committee on Social Trends, where he decided to carry out a study on the trend toward consumerism, Ogburn wanted Lynd to follow a method that was different from Lynd's own. The senior sociologist wanted to focus the research on the changes in consumer habits shown in the biannual census on the manufacture of products, and changes in lifestyle. Meanwhile, Lynd targeted his interest on the causes of such changes and the factors conditioning them; he was more interested in the motivations of the consumer than in the quantities consumed.

Lynd had observed firsthand in Muncie/Middletown that making money and "getting a living" were the two principles that dominated life there, and in America in general. Along with his collaborator, Alice Hanson, Lynd undertook what would become a controversial study: an extensive analysis of advertising, meant to determine how the advertising of products came about, the amount of money spent on advertising, and the types of advertising completed. Lynd wanted to propose the establishment of a government-sponsored consumer department that would do for the consumer what the Department of Commerce did for the business world.

Even before seeing the first drafts, Ogburn advised Lynd that he must make the research "as pure a scientific proposition as the social disciplines could permit." When the article came out, Ogburn's fears were confirmed: although it contained much real research, accompanied by fifty-two pages of footnotes and bibliography, the study not only did not advance concrete proposals, but also criticized a government agency, the Bureau of Standards. Lynd found an ally in Alice Hamilton, a professor of medicine at Harvard, who had just joined the committee. She supported the validity of the researcher's conclusions; her only criticism of Lynd's writing was that he should have criticized the Bureau of Standards more forcefully. All of this served to enlarge the debate, but Lynd's position won out and popular interest in the theme of consumerism was stimulated.

Robert's main interest in the 1930's was the attitude of the consumer. The Middletown scholar used Veblen's terminology, condemning American society at the time as a "money culture": people made money rather than things and accumulated property through financial manipulation rather than by working (M. C. Smith 1979–80). The continual pressure exerted on the individual to buy goods for consumption acted as a means whereby "superficial values tend[ed] to eliminate the values which express and represent human experience in the deepest and most subtle way" (R. S. Lynd 1957).

With a certain pessimistic anxiety, Lynd foresaw the future increase of consumerism and of consumer society as a whole. Here as well, Lynd followed one of Dewey's basic ideas: man, for the most part, is a creature of habit; the incessant repetition of messages tends to exclude any rational decision making. Lynd even came to doubt that "consumer demand" existed independently of the publicity and "style" created by industry. He then developed a program like the "Lynd Report," which proposed, among other things, the establishment of a body with legal authority and having the task of establishing standards for all products sold to the consumer. The sociologist insisted that the education of the consumer was impossible without the definition of a standard: the consumer may be able to distinguish between prices, but this means nothing if the product's quality is not defined (R. S. Lynd 1934). He became such a defender of standardizing the definition of quality that during his visit to the Soviet Union in 1938, he even tried to convince the planning committee of the Academy of Sciences to adopt the principle.

According to Lynd's own account, the committee representative told Lynd "calmly but firmly" that they did not consider this validation necessary in a "popular democracy" (R. S. Lynd 1954). Despite the best efforts of the activist-scholar, the establishment of a government-sponsored consumer department gradually came to nothing. Together with his collaborators, he subsequently turned to the establishment of agencies and organizations founded on popular support and became vice president of the Consumer's National Federation. The consumer movement was important for the development of Lynd's thinking in several ways. His experiences at Elk Basin (the oil camp) and in Middletown had made it clear to him that it was crucial to the work of an active sociologist to understand the "real" wishes and needs of the individual in a changing society (Thomas 1923).[7]

Middletown: Second Attempt

Robert returned to Muncie (this time without Helen) in 1935, more experienced and better "equipped" sociologically. He had it in mind to write an appendix, an updating of *Middletown*. In 1937, however, he produced a second whole volume (signed by both Robert and Helen), five hundred pages long, based on "new" data and on his own emerging interests. (When the editor Harcourt insisted on a second best-seller, and even suggested a third, after the great success of the first [Hoover 1990], Lynd replied that two books more than adequately exploited one single city.)

In the first volume, the two young researchers had emphasized the problems of a social system increasingly based on pecuniary values, and exhorted the inhabitants to resist them. *Middletown in Transition* revealed a process of manipulation completed not only in the area of consumption, but in other areas of life as well. Robert Lynd had become very critical of Middletown's—and America's—economic, political, and social institutions. His interest in the values of the individual brought him to admit, not without a certain bitterness, that the average Munsonian or Middletowner was becoming contemptibly passive in the face of domination by the business class and by its ever more powerful elite. As Lynd would say in his courageous depiction of the "spirit" of Middletown, the typical inhabitant of Muncie/Middletown did not want to have too much to think about. He or she was wholly satisfied to be left in peace, wrapped and protected by the often thick layer of indifference that by now enveloped the city: to think simply as he or she had been instructed to think.

Twice in *Middletown in Transition*, he expressed the fear that the middle class in Muncie, the "white collar" or "new" class, and the little business-men were ripe for a political regime such as fascism.[8] The only sign of hope that the Lynds were able to discern in Muncie of 1935 was the feeble attempt by the government to establish institutions that were in the best interest of the public. The Lynds believed in an organized system that left no space for speculation and individual irrationality; they deluded themselves that at the local level the federal government would intervene to establish a program for a return to American culture. They were not nostalgic for the lost world of the pioneers, but they nonetheless believed that America was at a crucial turning point. The values of self-direction and ethics that had driven the nation to create great cities and to construct a coherent culture (Berger and Luckmann 1966) was at risk of being annihilated by the advent of an irrational mass society in which democracy was only the facade of an anonymous, easily manipulated "solitary crowd" (Riesman 1950). Solidarity was disappearing without leaving other values in its place.

Even in Muncie, there was a kind of "straining for normality" that has been identified as a "typical element in other community studies" (Vidich and Bensman 1958). In this regard, Dahrendorf points out:

The individual conforms to this "pressure for normality" by repressing his/her own internal and external conflicts and by making use of the social-psychological technique of "externalization of the ego" in order to overcome his or her problems: through feverish activity, toil, and ritualization of behavior, but above all, through sociability, or rather, through that perception of community which the person imposes upon himself or herself precisely because he or she considers it normal to do so. (Dahrendorf 1959: 86)

The second series of research on the city showed that compulsory conformity and uniformity constituted the major features of the "Middletown spirit."

POWER AS REALITY

This pessimistic scenario was not only the product of a "cultural" transformation induced by growing consumption; actually, research into the subjects and objects of consumption, including hidden persuaders (Packard 1958), had sensitized Lynd to what would become his dominant theme: power. In *Middletown* he demonstrated the domination of the business class over the working class—which was strongly divided—and he was little worried about who made decisions, or how they were made, or whether they were advantageous to certain groups or individuals. His studies of psychological manipulation by advertising, and of the constant attempt on the part of industry to obtain ever greater profits without any interest in the individual, would bring him to recognize the fundamental meaning of control and power in American life. In *Middletown in Transition* he intended to demonstrate the new monopolistic forms of capitalistic organization. Industry and the politicians that sustained it, he maintained, were immeasurably stronger than consumers and their organizations.

This new perspective did not negate the earlier one, but rather was superimposed upon it. Muncie now appeared to be completely controlled from on high, by a real "royal family," "the X's"—the venturesome Ball brothers, who had arrived in Muncie at the time of the burgeoning of the gas business during the years overlapping the two centuries and had established low-cost industries. In a few decades, the Ball family had come to dominate the entire city and had gained control not only of the economy, but also of political and cultural life. The generous philanthropy of which they were proud was nothing more than a way of exercising control. The Lynds wrote (though Helen did not come with her husband to Muncie this time either) that there was no "personal malevolence" in the Balls' domination. Their powerful influence on the city was more unconscious than deliberate, but was nevertheless effective. The face of power was no longer fully hidden. A new reality was unmasked for the reader of Middletown.

COMMUNITY POWER: ELITISM OR PLURALISM?

The Lynds' position in *Middletown in Transition* provoked wide debate—which can be only briefly mentioned here—about the forms of local power. Students of politics were especially involved, particularly those interested in community power as well as in the Muncie story. It is easy to see, on the Lynds' side, a methodological, interpretative oversimplification about the nature of power in Middletown.

They proposed that a city of almost fifty thousand inhabitants was ruled by a socioeconomic oligarchy that revolved around the five Ball brothers. Their second study introduced the theory of elitism, whereby a small group of influential notables and tightly connected businessmen manipulated local affairs behind the scenes. Their categorization of the elite as part of the definition of community power (Warner 1959; Warner et al. 1963; Hunter 1953; Vidich and Bensman 1958) was the one most in vogue among scholars at that time and during the following decade. One of the most famous challenges to the guiding concept of elitism was the "pluralistic" paradigm put forth by Dahl (1961), who maintained that a community is not governed by a single elite, but rather by opposing interests and lobbies who participate in politics because of problems that relate directly to themselves. This results in an abdication of leadership responsibility, with the consequence that no one really "directs" a community (Lowry 1965). More recently, another model of decision making at the local level has emerged: the idea that "centralization" sustains the most important decisions in the community (Martindale and Hanson 1969; Elazar 1970), which are not determined by either local elites or pressure groups. Solutions to citizens' problems are encouraged, stimulated, and reinforced by agencies or authorities that are outside the community—namely, the state and the federal government.

Combined, the centralistic and the pluralistic versions can provide an alternative model to the one used by the Lynds in the 1930's to describe the relationship of community power to elitist power. There was no group in Muncie during those years that was able to exercise energetic, coherent influence on the local government (Frank 1979): very often the decision-making process ran aground when opposing factions disagreed and were unable to formulate solutions. Outside intervention became an obvious, even justified necessity because of the impotence of the local government.

Frank recalls three problems of particular importance to Muncie in the 1930's: the controversy over the municipal airport, the disagreement about financing public-works projects, and the endless discussion about the pollution of the river and what, if any, treatment should be required to clean it up. The pattern of these three events has convinced several different scholars that the X family had never exercised the massive power portrayed by the Lynds. It is even arguable that the family's power at the time was already in decline. Communities like Muncie were not isolated city-states, but were part of a larger and more complex political system (M. Stein 1960). They did not appear to constitute the privileged "reign" of any local elite, however influential.

Nonetheless, despite the validity of this criticism, the Lynds' theory of community power was used afterward in research by other scholars. An authoritative student of politics (Polsby 1960) has noted that those who research communities are inclined toward four basic interpretations: (1) to consider businessmen as a power elite and to ignore the role of politicians, so that in some studies only the former are interviewed; (2) to perceive power as a series of furtively exercised actions; (3) to treat power as a unitary, stable "thing" that is found at the top of the social structure and does not serve as a decentralizing element; and finally, (4) to view power as amorphous, determined by the situation, shared, changeable, or sporadically activated. A reexamination of the categories to use in studies on community power was therefore welcome. Along with criticism came proposed alternatives for the old group of theories that were so broadly and often so uncritically used in community studies.

THE X FAMILY: BETWEEN LEGEND AND HISTORY

Here the "history" of Muncie/Middletown ends and the "legend" begins. Doubts and questions remain about the impact that the X family, the Balls, actually had on the government of Muncie. Any reader of the first book on Middletown might well ask: why were the Balls never mentioned there? In the second book, the crucial presence of the X family is almost revelatory, like a rabbit pulled out of a hat. Recently, on the occasion of the Middletown III project directed by Theodore Caplow, controversy was stirred by the Lynds' "discovery" (or not) of the importance of the Balls. Robert Merton (1980) also contributed to the matter, as will be seen in Chapter 4.

What happened between the Lynds' first and second readings of the sociological and political map of Muncie? The Ball brothers were not only already operating, but were certainly already powerful in the middle of the 1920's. Why do the authors not even so much as name them or refer to them? Or perhaps, did someone point out to the Lynds the Balls' importance only after the first set of research?[9] There are no easy answers. The response of one scholar (Fox 1983) is convincing; he maintained that the Lynds became aware too late of the domination of the Balls in Muncie during their first research. This new perspective would have made the choice of Muncie "atypical," and therefore would have invalidated the "averageness" of Muncie, necessitating another choice. It is also true that during the 1930's, with the consolidation of the transition from competitive capitalism to monopolistic capitalism, an important family like the Balls would have stood out more clearly and commanded more attention than before. Nonetheless, it is certain that this second set of research has become part of the canon of sociology because of its treatment of a potentially controversial subject. In any case, these two chapters, "The X Family" and "The Spirit of Middletown," constituted the most conspicuous items in the narrative scheme of *Middletown in Transition*.

The structure of this second volume is substantially the same as that of the first; it examines six categories of changes that occurred during the decade: "getting" a living, making a home, training the young, using leisure, engaging in religious practices, engaging in community activities. Without the chapters "The X Family" and "The Spirit of Middletown," the second study would probably be considered today only a modest, though interesting, addendum to the first.

The Reconstruction of Knowledge

Both Lynds were well aware that the American problem went beyond the dilemma of power and social inequality, which they felt could not be resolved at the local level or attributed to a single "nucleus" or elite. As they affirmed in the last pages of the first volume on Middletown, American society had to be reformed. Continuing to act the part of the scholar engaged in the solution of real problems, Robert Lynd searched for solutions in other political realities: thus his trip with Helen to the Soviet Union in search of "understanding" and his book *Knowledge for What?* are in a sense a double testimony to the direction his research was taking. While Helen would choose the way of social psychology,[10] Robert would take another direction, more or less predictable even in its premature interruption.

Most leftist American intellectuals during the 1930's had come to have an ever more negative view of the Soviet experiment and an ever more positive one of the New Deal. Lynd, however, did the opposite: he began as an active supporter of the New Deal in the 1930's and came to defend the Soviet experiment at the end of the decade. He remained positively impressed by what he had seen in the Soviet Union in 1938 and regarded the Soviet experiment as a genuine effort to avoid the two extremes of total control, typified by the Nazis, or of organized confusion, such as he found at the roots of local life in America. "Time would prove that, despite our present greater liberties, only the Soviet Union among the great modern nations is laying the foundations for fundamental liberties" (1939a).

When Lynd spoke of liberty, he meant appropriate, regulated, useful social activity. Social "liberty" and subjective "liberty" were never separate for Lynd; they were too important to be left to chance or to the caprice of individual choice. Broader power for social scientists would act as a guarantee against irresponsibility and consequent disorder, and would also prevent society from deteriorating into authoritarianism. He explained these ideas in *Knowledge for What?* (1939), appropriately subtitled *The Place of Social Science in American Culture*. Lynd perceived that the "sociological institution" itself posed three principal obstacles to the potentially profitable exchange between sociologist and culture: the cult of "theory," overspecialization in academia, and the formation of a kind of "scientific priesthood." Social problems had come to be examined only within the framework of academic disciplines and on the basis of special interests, rather than in accordance with the criteria of social utility.

CAUGHT IN THE WHIRLPOOL

Robert Lynd felt that social research should not be guided by the mere curiosity of the researcher, nor carried out for the satisfaction of a small intellectual coterie that dedicated itself to knowledge for its own sake. Social scientists should, above all, "foster action" instead of simply completing analyses and drawing conclusions. Lynd maintained that social scientists, no more than other scientists, should be held responsible for formulating practical, moral, or aesthetic judgments. As mere human beings, they must not only define and foresee the consequences of one political choice or another, but they must exercise "social responsibility" and its influence on people and their courses of action. There is a famous expression of Lynd with regard to scholars who continue debating even in the face of disaster, "lecturing on navigation while the ship is going down." In the spirit of Pascal's metaphor "Vous êtes embarqué," Lynd condemns the social scientists not so much for their science, but for their ethics: their detachment from human affairs and their indifference toward their neighbor's "shipwreck" (Blumenberg 1997). Here, disagreement among social scientists came to include many different points of view: for example, "to debate about the route" when the vessel—the common culture or a person's own life—is going down, might communicate interesting information about navigation and its dangers, even though allowing those onboard, the "fishermen," to be trapped in the whirlpool (Elias 1988).

With such practical considerations unaddressed (the third way of Mannheim?), *Knowledge for What?* was not destined for success. According to recent commentators (Coser 1986), the work appeared too late to have a real impact, and today communicates a sense of déjà vu: it was an excess of radicalism that suggested its utopian appeal. Lynd was a *sociologue engagé*: he related problems in sociology to decision making in order to make an effective contribution to the emancipation of humankind.

The work of the young Robert and the work of the mature Robert invite reflection even today on the "cultural contradictions" (Bell and Boudon 1978) that limit the growth of the modern world. In their universal approach to culture, the Lynds never believed in an ascetic system of ideas, in an "archaeology of knowledge" (Foucault 1971) that they interpreted as overspecialization, fragmentation, and bureaucratization of the social sciences. In their opinion, this would favor an ever easier manipulation by the capitalistic system as well as an ever more precise and minute analysis of banal problems ("learning more and more about less and less").

The two works on Middletown were meant to demystify research. The immediacy of the problems and the urgency of their interpretation in a "living" context was the advantage. In his empirical research, Lynd was able to touch on the perverse mix of contradictory cultural traits present and emerging in the mind and heart of the "average" American citizen. It is Lynd's theorization afterward that is unconvincing and that is inconsistent with his convictions and with history itself; it reveals flaws in methodology and interpretation that were much easier to forgive in his great undertaking of community research. Not by chance is *Knowledge for What?* criticized from many points of view. In fact, the twelve "outrageous theories" formulated at the end of the book, as Lazarsfeld remembers (1971), had the character of a direct provocation for Columbia's and other sociology departments. Criticism arrived from as far away as Frankfurt (Horkheimer 1947). Horkheimer did not look favorably on Lynd's mixture of "reason" and "action": critical thought must be used to demystify reality, not to suggest solutions. In addition, he maintained that the energies that scientists dedicate to reflection must not be deviated into action.[11]

Other scholars believe that Horkheimer's criticism does not do justice to Lynd's ideas about the ongoing conflict that pits human being against human being, class against class, and that, even today, "frustrates the deep human need to collaborate toward a common end or general good, which is a fundamental condition of that society that Lynd reasonably and defensibly outlines." Lynd wanted a planned and unified democratic society, and believed that the conditions necessary for producing this resided in the moral and psychological domains, in certain human needs and predispositions that needed to be cultivated and strengthened with education, information, and "rite" (Cavalli 1970b).

It should not be forgotten that the Lynds' trip to Russia was a social and political adventure destined to leave strong traces on Robert's perception of society. He thought that certain elements of socialism could be introduced into America, but at the same time, he believed in certain basic values of American democracy that had to be salvaged to produce a society that would be antitotalitarian but "democratically" controlled.

FEAR OF POWER

In a letter from Riesman to Lynd in 1939, Riesman refers to a proposal by Lynd that either reveals a "Rousseau touch" or even contradicts other parts of his thought—or both. In Lynd's "political" proposals at least two traits can be perceived: a certain utopianism, of course, but also a certain incoherence in his denouncement of capitalistic power. How could a group of intellectuals oppose such an omnipotent system that conditioned all of American culture? Seen through *Middletown in Transition*, that conditioning appeared overwhelmingly irreversible.

The power exercised by the X family was total and left no room for the authors to imagine any type of individual or collective initiative. The Lynds described the forms of control exercised by the Balls in the educational institutions and in the mass media as a kind of "needs-based dictatorship." Could Middletown ever return to a non-denatured human nature? It is not really clear whether Lynd was merely guilty of wishful thinking, or was actually considering strategies of social action in which, as Merton says, the relationship of means to ends was reestablished.

The mature Robert would attempt to confront and write about the problem of the multifaceted face of capitalist power that assumed an ever more phantasmagoric character for him. But his thinking never reaches completion. His attempts to write on the subject (foreword to Robert Brady's *Business as a System of Power*, 1943; and "Power in American Society," 1957) have a provisional character: they deferred a more complete analysis that was never concluded. The "great" research on power in America outlined by Lynd and discussed with Robert Merton would never be brought to term. He was trapped in his sociological imagination. He would become ever more intolerant in his criticism, even of those who were closest to him (Izzo 1977), such as C. Wright Mills and David

Riesman: Mills because of his *The Power Elite* (1956), where Lynd perceived a theory of the elite that ignored the real mechanisms of inequality at all levels of American society and thus was a kind of alibi for his lack of purpose and political activism (R. S. Lynd 1956) Disagreement with Riesman was less direct, but the rupture between the two was no less forceful. It should be remembered that, while for Lynd the manipulative power of the capitalistic system was manifested in all its perversity in the world of consumption, Riesman perceived it as an imperfect way to more social equality. He would even move one step further and ask (1969): Why abundance? Why do we need abundance? in a society presumed to be beyond scarcity (Kolko 1981).

ESTRANGEMENT

With the arguments brought forth in *Knowledge for What?*, Lynd had reached the final logical point of his social analysis and of his intellectual development. *Middletown* constituted a strong attack on the consumer culture, an eloquent condemnation of the passivity to which citizens seemed to be condemned. *Middletown in Transition* broke with the earlier view, which was in many ways nostalgic for good old American values, in order to "view" the irrationality of the people who were subject to manipulation by organized, capitalistic, unscrupulous people. Lynd never gave up disdaining the hedonistic ethic of consumerism. Like his idol, Thorstein Veblen, he detested the idea that life was "conspicuous," that it could be conceived as mere consumption and waste. He hoped for a more moral, productive life, rigorous like that of the men and women belonging to the Protestant America of the last years of the preceding century. Given his renunciation of every transcendental reference, Lynd resigned himself to the fact that there could never be a satisfying social solution.

During the 1930's, Lynd was more and more intimidated by the increasing cleverness of the younger generation of sociologists and the so-called decreasing quality of research (Ferrarotti 1989).[12] When Lazarsfeld entered Columbia in 1940 at Robert's wish, he felt ever more inadequate among his colleagues. He was unable to complete either the two essays on the Depression that he had begun in the 1930's or the project on power in America that he would work on erratically during the 1950's and that both Lazarsfeld and his other great friend, Robert Merton, repeatedly but unsuccessfully urged him to complete. The brilliant researcher of Middletown had lost faith in his work.

He was frequently depressed, and though he continued to busy himself with "radical causes," he gradually retired from the intellectual arena. The image that he liked to evoke of himself was that of a reasonable, solitary man who brooded on "climbing over the hilltop and falling into oblivion on the other side without ever understanding what was wrong or why it was wrong" (R. S. Lynd 1954). Silence became for him the most dignified choice in "this world of loneliness" where he no longer felt at ease and where he had become a kind of "Homeless Mind" (Berger, Berger, and Kellner 1973).

CHAPTER 2

Middletown I: Eclipse of the Community

The Myth of the Small Town

The American mind and literary imagination are charmed by the idea of the small town as an ideal linked to the heroic world of the pioneers.[1] The works of such storytellers as Zona Gale (*Friendship Village*, 1908) and Willa Cather (*My Antonia*, 1918) show how irresistible and heartfelt these ideals were, not only for the writers who described them, but also for the people who lived in the Midwest at the turn of the century.

About this time, however, an awareness of certain other aspects of provincial life—its small-mindedness, its stereotyping, and its hypocrisies—began to emerge in the books of such major writers as Sherwood Anderson, Sinclair Lewis, and Edgar Lee Masters. But even they betrayed a certain ambivalence, reconstructing small-town life as the ever-reassuring and protective world from which they started. Edgar Lee Masters mythologizes his own background in *Hometown*, and Anderson's "poor white" is described with affection and nostalgia even though situated in a difficult context, where geniality, paradoxically, is born from poverty and marginality. Students of American literature have identified two opposing tendencies in these descriptions of small-town life, which in turn lead to several different conceptions of community: the "romantic," the "realistic," and the "idealized."

According to the "romantic" interpretation, the midwestern small town is a place

of economic well-being, neither cursed by poverty nor corrupted by wealth, where community solidarity and friendship prevail; where the middle class first took root, typically American, healthy, and human despite its prosaic limits; and where American democracy resides, dominated by the spirit of equality, according to which men are measured by their innate qualities.[2]

The "realistic" interpretation, however, emphasizes small-mindedness and competitiveness in reaction to "the acquisitive ideal of the civilization of the machine"; "the grand illusion of American civility, the illusion of optimism," which avoids reality and weakens intellectual fiber; and the inhibitions of a Puritanism that has lost its own sanctions.[3]

Booth Tarkington, a native of Indiana and author of *Hoosier*, typifies the writer with an "idealized" vision of the American town. His two best-known novels, *The Gentleman from Indiana* (1899) and *The Magnificent Amberson* (1918; film 1942), honor the middle-class virtues as well as the bourgeois quest for success—thus embodying the paradoxical, fundamental "cultural conflict" the Lynds struggled against.

THE REALITY OF THE GOOD YEARS

The "good years" referred to in many of these novels represent a distinct historical period having definite sociological characteristics. It commences at the end of the last century and lasts until the 1920's, before the turbulence and crises that would cause America to change its whole style of life. Documentation of the changes taking place in the small- to medium-sized cities that were reshaped by the great process of industrialization clearly linked those changes to structural transformation more than to cultural factors. During the 1930's, American writers' references to community appeared to assume—though with some misgiving—that the "good years" were past.

But it was a sociologist's work, not a literary figure's (though the work was certainly well written), that denounced the changes in the American provinces resulting from the rush to industrial organization—first the "boom," then the "bust." The victories of science and technology had shattered the sense of community, leaving space only for narrow-minded, irrational individualism. The false promises of consumption, with the consequent rendings in the social fabric and breaches in solidarity, blighted all hopes and dreams. The past had become myth in the individual imagination as well as in collective memory. The time had come to investigate what had happened over those few decades and what sort of person had emerged with the advent of the machine age and the successes of industrialization (Friedmann 1946).

The historical development of these changes was documented in sociological and anthropological detail by the Lynds in their narrative depiction of "Middletown." Published in 1929, the year of the great economic crisis, the study of Muncie, Indiana, represented the scientific counterpart of the literary depiction of Bidewell, Ohio, by Sherwood Anderson. Anderson was interested in individual reactions to the great transformations taking place (Nisbet 1957), while the Lynds were more interested in gather-

ing information on changes in the diverse social institutions, collective behavior, and the contrasting interests of different socioeconomic classes.

A remarkable increase in population was the fundamental indicator of
transformation. It was precisely this process that the Lynds wished to take
into account as they declared in the first pages of their text:

> We are coming to realize, moreover, that we today are probably living in one of the
> eras of greatest rapidity of change in the history of human institutions. New tools
> and techniques are being developed with increasing rapidity, while in the wake of
> these technical developments increasingly frequent and strong culture waves sweep
> over us from without, drenching us with the material and non-material habits of
> other centers. In the face of such a situation it would be a serious defect to omit
> this developmental aspect from a study of contemporary life.[4]

The critical perspective adopted by the Lynds shows how social
changes and changes in the organization of work were evoked by industrialization, eventually extending to include all aspects of human activity,
until finally the individual was overwhelmed. The two courageous young
authors highlighted the negative consequences, while nostalgically looking back to lost values. They became firmly convinced that the consequences of standardization and the impersonalization of industrial work
were disastrous, and that the social and personal price was extremely high.
The worker's decline in status, the increased rigidity of class divisions, the
decreased opportunity for social mobility—all of this needed to be denounced, at whatever the cost.

The Lynds believed that "progress" led from solidarity to solitude, both
at work and in the community, where no new values took the place of the
old ones. In their first research on Middletown, the year 1890 was taken
as the focal point of the "good years," after which so many transformations took place.[5] The Lynds asked questions about what had changed and
why the changes created new, unremitting inequalities among people. The
young critics, however, did not focus just on the mythical year 1890
(Turner [1920] 1976), but also projected a "possible" utopian future that
would deny the supremacy of the "business-first attitude."[6] Theirs was a
nostalgia that looked back to the time when the community was still a
strong social institution; and it was a hope that looked forward to a better
future.

AMBIVALENCE IN THE COMMUNITY

The study of community and the social mechanisms linked to it are important to sociology; in fact, the model-community paradigm is central to
the thought of at least three great "classical" founding fathers of sociology:
Durkheim, Max Weber, and Toennies.

We shall refer especially to Toennies in the pages that follow because his work specifically treats the contrast between community and society, as well as the ambiguity contained in the concept of community. Toennies regretted the loss of the simple way of life, which was destined to be overwhelmed by the fatal expansion of industrial mass society, and by the consequent depersonalization, individualism, competitiveness, and crisis of values that it involved.[7] The German sociologist was convinced of the necessity of recovering human associations that were based on mutual acceptance and not on the "cold," calculating criteria of a technological society. Without abstracting the ideal of harmonious community into an impracticable utopia, Toennies's ideas identified (in the spirit of the Chicago School of sociology) the processes of interdependence among the various areas of society. He provided no practical information, however, about how to live in modern terms in solidarity with one's fellows, and not just in conservative regret.[8] The Toenniesian contrast between community and society suggested the impossibility of finding new channels of fulfillment and community association, given the inevitability of modernization.

It might be pertinent here to touch briefly on certain essential points of Toennies's thought, in order to understand his ideas about the contrast between community and society, and to reduce their ambivalence—an ambivalence from which not even the Lynds are exempt. For Toennies "community" is characterized by a deep, natural solidarity that is based not so much on rationality as on consensus, harmony, and empathy—a shared destiny in both good and bad times. "Society," on the other hand, is based on rational objectives that are attainable through specific means. Reciprocal actions by individuals rest on definite, "neutral" expectations that do not necessarily involve the affections. While members of society reach accord through negotiation, members of the community are interdependent. In these terms, Durkheim will refer to the types of mechanical and organic solidarity.

Statements of Toennies, such as the following, show that his preference for community reflected the intellectual climate of Germany in 1887: "Dialectical juxtaposition is not the exception, but the rule. Think, as just one example, of the Dionysus-Apollo antinomy of F. Nietzsche's *Birth of Tragedy*, in 1872" (Giannotti 1977: 527). In addition, one can find in the community-society contrast

the tendency to identify absolutely with the original German *Geist* which opposes French rationalism and English utilitarianism, the romantic idealization of Medieval society. . . . Neither must one forget that Toennies felt strongly Marx's influence, especially regarding his interpretation of the destructive attributes of bourgeois revolution with respect to more traditional feelings and human relationships.[9]

Toennies's interest in and attachment to the theme of community can be explained also in terms of his biography. As a descendent of a farming family of many generations, he was naturally attracted by a sense of community and came to accept socialism because of his spontaneous feeling toward the working class,

which is the one that most conserves community spirit and possesses a livelier and more sincere sense of morality and social justice. This explains why he often insisted in the book from which this quote is taken, and in his successive works, on the importance of community spirit and on the moral exigencies that ought to inspire a workers' movement; and why he did not withhold criticism against Marxism for having set aside the moral imperatives that contrasted with Marxism's belief in the gradual effects of economic processes and the inevitable ascendancy of the working class.[10]

This "preference" is expressed linguistically in the series of opposites that are implied by *Gemeinschaft* and *Gesellschaft*: organic, "real" life versus ideal, "mechanical" life; the "hot impulses of the heart" in contrast to the cold intellect; and above all—in accordance with the Germanic *Geist*—land-bound farmers contrasted to the solid middle class of industrialists and unscrupulous shopkeepers attached to their work and hidebound in selfishness.

In Toennies's own words:

Every common form of human association is community; society, on the other hand, is the public, the world. We find ourselves in community from birth and are linked to it through good and bad times, and we venture into society as if it were a foreign land. A young person is put on guard against bad company, but "a bad community" is contrary to the sense of the language . . . and human society is understood as the pure coexistence of people who are independent from one another. Community is ancient, whereas society is new. . . . Community is long-lasting and genuine; society will pass away.[11]

The intent of Toennies is not so much to develop a theory of society as to posit a theory of community. The German sociologist took on himself the task of conceptual clarification, enrichment, and consolidation of the theoretical bases of nascent sociology.[12] Toennies's antagonistic stance has been weakened, diluted, and modernized in the various editions and versions that his work has undergone, which place emphasis not on the renewal of the community, but on its integration into the structures of industrial and postindustrial society.

THE ONGOING NEED FOR COMMUNITY

The Lynds agreed with the classical perspective on the "passage" from community to society, although they disliked capitalist society, which is based on mass consumption.

After the Second World War, the theme of "mass society" would be developed with greater force and community's problems would once again be examined. It was a subject that would continue to influence and attract researchers, many of whom would underscore the contrast between the cohesive influence of community and the alienating effects of large-scale social organization. They would denounce (Riesman 1950) the emergence of the "other-directed" personality, who must submit to the negative pressure of mass society and then be condemned to loneliness in the "crowd." There is an echo here of de Tocqueville's "tyranny of the majority" at democracy's heart, which he believed was destined ultimately to undermine democracy altogether.

Thus, in the Lynds' wake, the critical link between mass society and urban society was reformulated:

Urban life . . . tends to create solitary beings, to uproot the individual from his habits of life, to pit him against the social void, to weaken traditional checks on personal behavior. . . . In our civilization, with its values of faith in oneself and self-sufficiency, surrounded by relationships which become even more impersonal and by authorities which become ever more remote, there is the incipient tendency . . . toward a growing sense of solitude and uncertainty.[13]

As a result, individuals isolated within their own contexts search for unlikely solutions in their private lives—in marriage and in family— thereby overburdening already strained and complex relationships. Communal needs reemerge, therefore, in religious participation, in "family values" and personal relationships, love itself becoming "a haven in a heartless world" (Lasch 1977)—all painful attempts to compensate in private life for the problems and defects of public life (Hirschman 1983; Bellah et al. 1985).

The Lynds' research in Muncie would reveal problems that were important to both individual and collective well-being: the decline of family relationships and of the neighborhood in the local community, and the failure of new social structures to provide satisfactory substitutes. The Lynds' empirical investigation into the effects of mass industrialization led them to condemn the emerging egotistical mentality that valued business above collective well-being.

The real problem was not really so much the loss of the old contexts, but rather, the incapacity of the democratic, industrial environment to create new, morally cohesive social contexts within which a person's minor loyalties assume a functional and psychological meaning. What caused this failure? The problem was normally attributed to the impact of technology or to city life; but those realities were not necessarily incompatible with the moral values and social relationships that for modern people replace the family, parish, and village relationships so essential to people in the past.

The theme of the demise of traditional authorities and the resulting void in mass society is one that would return in the 1950's in the writings of the exponents of North American "critical sociology."[14] The Lynds were precursors in their censure of the dysfunction and negative values in American society and culture before the Second World War.[15] Their work examined developing phenomena that would reach full expression in the years following the war. The withering of social and human relationships resulted in inequality and injustice, and in an impoverishment of the subjective personality and its withdrawal in the face of "repressive tolerance" (Marcuse 1968b). The Lynds were among the first critical sociologists; they were pioneers in facing the fundamental, knotty problems of the "affluent society" (Galbraith 1958), and in trying to find solutions to these problems.

THE COEXISTENCE OF COMMUNITY AND SOCIETY

Research of community appears to correspond, therefore, to a profound desire inherent in human nature, "a need for a clear sense of cultural finality, material prosperity, social order and continuity. Without these, no material prosperity of any sort will serve to arrest our society's growing sense of alienation and the needs of the community."[16]

Community, in other words, is an archaic, elemental, and basic antidote for the ancestral fear of silence, isolation, and obscurity. It fulfills the need to reconstruct an "accessible" world from which the "outsider" (Schutz 1971) is barred. Communal relationship—whether it involves detachment from or reconciliation to something forgotten—is a favorite theme of the human sciences. The desire for a familiar, protective place implies a regressive element that the need for community also tends to express: a nostalgic streak, a backward motion. The realization of this need, if insufficiently prepared for and worked out, can eventually assume an agitated, disturbing quality.

Nostalgia for strong community roots can become very conservative; in social criticism, the researcher must look beyond the mere recovery of lost human ties. As Nisbet affirms in agreement with Robert Lynd, the problem does not lie in the loss of old contexts, but rather in the incapacity of the modern, democratic, industrial environment to create new contexts of moral and social cohesion. In the absence of a new system of loyalties, *Middletown* delineates the passage from old community values to anomic confusion; new values are proposed with which to start anew after a systematic, collective action.[17] Thus, the old, forgotten contrast between community and society is reformulated in its Toenniesian version, exasperatingly excluding one or the other of the two terms.

It has been noted recently that community reproduces itself.[18] Far from excluding or choosing one or the other, contemporary people actually live in both worlds, that of the *Gemeinschaft* and that of the *Gesellschaft*. And it is precisely this sort of rich, complex personality that traverses more worlds of life (Berger and Berger 1973). The opposition between community and society, between the intimate, family world and the impersonal, "empty" world is thus less marked; and thus it becomes more possible to reevaluate both public and private life.

THE TYRANNY OF THE MACHINE

The Lynds examined the problems concerning the relationship of community to industrialization. During the twenties and thirties, these themes were explored as well by other social critics such as Stuart Chase: nostalgia for community, criticism of industrialization, and careful planning of technological developments were the only ways to guarantee that modern material conquests would not be used corruptly.

Explicitly connected to the Lynds' work, on which he enthusiastically commented, Chase is a typical representative of those who referred to community nostalgically. His writings mainly express the idea that industrial society can never meet the expectations of such nostalgia.[19] Chase criticizes the ideology of "business first," as described in *Middletown* by the Lynds, and characterizes the average business man as a savage shark-profiteer who monopolizes technological advances.

Chase looks at the "nostalgic" past in order to compare it to the present. For example, the life of one of Chase's grandfathers in Newburyport, Massachusetts, who had lived almost a century before him, suggests that the quality of life, food, and habits had degenerated rather than improved.

But what indicators does Chase use for the model of life that he has in mind? One problem he examines is the discrepancy between income and real, material conditions. His grandfather's income as a farmer, Chase argues, was average for his community, while Chase's own income added to that of his wife was probably three times the average income for the city in which he lived. Other indicators Chase considers include habitation, neighborhood, and urban construction—none of which, in his opinion, demonstrate a century of progress. Finally—and this was a pet peeve of social critics of that time—the so-called advantages of machines that could substitute for hundreds of human arms and produce such larger quantities of goods, seemed to be continually postponed—until they appeared to be *dis*advantages.

Chase argued with conviction about that now outdated topic, the delusion of the machine. Even the foreseen economic advantages that it was supposedly bringing, he argued, did not meet expectations. Science and technology were not in themselves disadvantageous; the excessive freedom allowed to economic liberalism had nullified the benefits of industrialization and, as a result, the quality of life in the community had not improved, but had actually worsened. Greedy profiteering in business did not take into consideration the economic planning that would have been advantageous to the community.

Doubtless, argued Chase in this regard, certain needs are best provided for by private initiative, and others by specific groups in the community. There was no reason to believe that there was only one way of managing the economy of the whole country for 116 million people. All dogmas had their own risks: from absolute liberty in business at one extreme, to state socialism at the other. At this point in time the third way, represented by planning, was the least tried.

The lack of planning for the community and the region was the main factor responsible for the dispersion of energy. New cities, continued Chase, often rose in inappropriate places where there had never been a home in which people discovered beauty, happiness, rest, and faith—they were places where men and women simply worked hard, ate, and slept. Of the great American cities, for example, only Washington had been planned with comfortable living in mind, above and beyond builders' economic speculation. On the other hand, it was not easy to break the siege of the world of profit, to make technology operate for the good of the community. This would be a betrayal of the business principle, and so was unthinkable.

An example of a place where the ideology of business-first held sway was the Lynds' Middletown. Chase refers in this regard to the key chapter in the Lynds' book, "Why Do They Work So Hard?" Chase's question is simple but basic: why does the amount of time that people dedicate to themselves never diminish when they are provided with energy, machines, and labor-saving devices? These devices should, in fact, translate into more rest, more tranquillity, more security. In reality, the people of Middletown never cease working because they have been taught to want more and more things, and thus to work more to obtain their desires—thereby losing a sense of gratification in their work. It was true that machines had increased production and reduced the time necessary to make a product—for example, in Muncie, the automobile—but keeping the automobile on the road required additional work that was not necessary before the automobile was invented.

In addition, among the problems intrinsic to the system of industrial production, another problem arose that was linked to the use of time. Paralleling the increase in work and production, the necessity for new goods grew and the downward spiral of compensation through consumption of the superfluous became more precipitous. Observation of the excessive industriousness of the Middletown population and the lack of time they had for themselves revealed that industrialization inflicted fatigue more than it encouraged a better quality of life.

Chase contrasts the "Middletown model" and the European agricultural village of the fourteenth century. Examining the two in an attempt to determine who worked more, who slept more, and who ate better shows that while the people in the village worked hard and long, they often had a series of holidays during which they entertained themselves at length. The men and women of Middletown worked fewer hours per day but were lucky if they had a single week of vacation annually—aside from Sundays and legal holidays. Even today the outside observer can plainly see that work and the monetary gain bound up with it are still central to the lives of the people of Middletown.

In Search of American Values

What exactly were the "American values" in question during the twenties and thirties in the United States that received the brunt of the Lynds' censure? Faith in humanitarian principles had been placed side by side with the creed of efficiency that was based on the idea of free competition. This is one way of formulating the dissociation between money-oriented attitudes and religiosity—the latter, according to de Tocqueville, being one of the strong points of the "American spirit."

In the theoretical work that immediately follows the two studies of Middletown, *Knowledge for What?* (1939), the Lynds argue that these deep needs that are at the heart of human nature (Thomas 1923) can be expressed in a democratic society only when the democracy is rationally planned; otherwise, they clash with the principles of ruthless competition—with all the resulting devastating effects on the individual and the group. The "price of civilization" (Freud 1929) for the individual is neurosis and insecurity (Horney 1955), which in turn come to be characterized as weaknesses to be used against the citizen. The industry of consumption is always ready to twist things to its own advantage.

The ideology and practice of consumerism were presented, in fact, as the one salvation in a world where promises of social advancement, of equal opportunity and fortune, were not kept and were replaced by new illusions authoritatively marketed as certainties (Bell and Boudon 1978): "free time" was an empty promise; the time available to individuals was taken away by the capitalistic demand for efficiency and high performance.

Spontaneous associations, the heritage of the great democratic tradition, disappeared in order to make way for ever more formal organizations. And thus community itself vanished, along with all that had constituted its "spirit": collective goals, the means adapted to achieve these, and the lack of waste; central values that in the last analysis encouraged collective well-being without taking anything away from individual welfare. The ideal of community as integration was referred to in literature and the common language; and it was the obverse of this ideal that the research in Middletown exposed.

But the Lynds' criticism of the "eclipse of community" did not just identify "cultural contradictions." Their denouncement of the all-encompassing capitalistic ideology and of the manipulation of conscience through consumption includes an espousal of other opposing values. Their criticism takes substance and strength from their empirical observation of life in an average American city. For the Lynds, "nostalgia for the community" was not wishing for the past, but rather the first move toward negation of the perverse tendencies of capitalistic society and toward identification of more rational and "noble" forms of living together.

MIDDLETOWN: A CRITICAL STUDY

The sociology of the young Lynds is an ingenious union of the theoretical criticism put forth by the European sociological "classics" and that advanced by the American social scientists of those years. Industrialism, *The Theory of the Leisure Class* (Veblen 1899), the "other-direction" (i.e., social behavior oriented toward the opinions of others; see Riesman 1950), "the power elite" (Mills 1956), and "planning"[20] were germinal concepts that were already circulating in American society between the two wars and that would later come to full maturity. These and similar ideas that were more or less related to the great critical tradition of European sociological thought, from Mannheim to Adorno, would come into their own in American intellectual circles.

With the contribution of the Lynds, moreover, criticism focused on the demise of the community and other phenomena linked to it. Their description of the various activities of daily life in a specific place in the industrialized Midwest represented the living demonstration of ideals and of departures from those ideals. On one hand, the Lynds' criticism was tempered by minute detail and analysis of particulars, and on the other, it was radical, extending to all areas of life and exposing the "typical" collective and individual tendency toward standardization and conformity.

Finally, their chosen method of entering unannounced into a social microcosm with identifiable characteristics (the "knowable community" of Stein [1960]) was ahead of their time, presaging Merton's "middle range theory" (Merton 1949). The choice of this method also opened up the possibility of *serendipity*, another Mertonian idea: more than once the Lynds confirmed "that one dissimilar datum stimulates the birth of theory" (Ibid.).

The Lynds' critical contribution to sociology becomes evident when placed within the context of the work of other contemporary scholars, such as C. Wright Mills and Lewis Coser, who saw society as an aggregate of poorly integrated economic, political, and educational institutions (Tumin 1987). In consequence, they saw property, power, and prestige as the exclusive privileges of a virtually inaccessible elite. Those excluded could not enjoy the good things of life. The social inequality propagated by the different strata, or classes, of society came to represent a source of fundamental conflict in society. This perspective of the so-called "critical sociologists" viewed conflict as an intrinsic, natural, and predictable feature of the organization of society. Alberto Izzo, the historian of Italian sociology, has commented that "despite the democratic facade, the restrictive aspects of American society are accentuated—its explicit violence, or at least its manipulativeness—and consequently its fundamentally antidemocratic character".[21]

Therefore, there is no doubt that the Lynds represented that fruitful critical tradition and radical propensity. Delving into the Lynds' research today is both stimulating and meaningful: their legacy represents the collective abundance of a group of pioneering intellectuals and scholars who were trained before the Second World War, and their work reached to the heart of certain problems in America at that time. Therefore, the thinking and the activities of the group, in accordance with the rich tradition of the sociology of knowledge, are historically identifiable and socially influenced, in an age marked by profound and sudden changes—the swings between well-being and crisis that characterized American capitalism between the two wars. By the twenties, the machine culture and the "civilization of consumption" had come to be rooted in the "affluent society" (Galbraith 1958) that expected the improvements brought about by progress to be extended ad infinitum—a society that did not want to see and confront its own contradictions.

The Lynds' *Middletown* acquired a revelatory power that provoked diverse reactions among its readership, which included a fairly large group of specialists, counterculture intellectuals, and also average Americans, those who saw the book in a shop window, and recognized how it described their values and problems: and so the book became a best-seller.

THE TYPICALNESS OF MUNCIE/MIDDLETOWN

In American mythology, "home" is an average city of about fifty thousand inhabitants and the best context for sentimental films set at the turn of the century. Although this type of setting came to be viewed ambivalently, its expression does signify the importance it had for American life. On one hand, this average city was seen as philistine, a fertile terrain for recruitment by the American Legion and a reign of bad taste. On the other hand, it represented the historical memory of pioneering America and the conquests and achievements from "nothing" of the early settlers. From the prairie and the desert were born the industrial cities that became living symbols of the technological leap of the new civilization.[22]

The Lynds chose Muncie, Indiana, because they believed it embodied the essence of American culture and institutions. Its "average" size, economic base, and demographic composition promised a valid representation of America between the two wars. Aside from methodological considerations, which we shall consider later, historical and social reasons also fully justified the choice. In the first half of the twentieth century, in fact, America was better represented by Muncie than by crowded urban centers or by declining rural areas. New York City and Chicago were still something else altogether, because of the type of populations present in those places and their general and specific characteristics. The "metropolis" extolled by Simmel was for most Americans still an extraneous reality, too heterogeneous, too cosmopolitan, too noisy, a place of violence and "vice." Even in literature, the romance of the urban environment—already widespread in Europe by the 1800's—was not fully developed in the United States until the thirties. Big-city sociology and the blossoming of the Chicago School emerged around the same time; however, it was not until the Second World War that the center of gravity in the social sciences moved definitively toward the metropolis. By then, it was evident that the American population, with the consolidation of the "melting pots" of cities such as New York and Chicago, lived ever more in big metropolitan centers. Therefore, new cultural models and values came from those places, and not from the static provinces. The contrasts and excesses of the metropolis, in Europe (Ilardi 1990) as well as America, became the dominant themes, but newly emerging potentials and identities were also noticed.

While it is quite clear that Muncie no longer represents the typical American city, if it ever did, both now and recently it represented a typical American city of the industrialized Midwest. There was and is no real "Middletown," but rather a series of middle-sized cities that are spread out over the nation and that are differentiated by economic base and demographic composition, and are more or less dependent on the major metropolitan areas.

For example, the ethnic homogeneity of the inhabitants of Middletown, which was taken by the Lynds as an index of "typical" rootedness in the original American stock—what Robert Lynd liked to call the "good old stock"—could not be assumed any more then than today. Interpretation of a "community" and the process of bringing that interpretation to life must not leave out those elements that are inconsistent with or that dispute its predefined characteristics. Rather than being fixated on a rigid "typicalness" that immobilizes classes, social orders, values, and lifestyles, it seems more useful to identify the characteristics of the context or group under study and their transformation in time along dynamic, identifiable coordinates. One example might be the community studies in the thirties of the phenomena of urbanization, industrialization, and bureaucratization. As Maurice Stein (1960) has noted, all three of the urban community studies that he investigated (Robert E. Park, Lloyd Warner, and Lynd and Lynd) give a lively picture of the vicissitudes of big and medium-sized cities during the twenties and thirties.

It is important to consider the historical events themselves that bear on the period under examination; the study of community is the study of the transformations occurring in it. In the words of Stein, "Every serious community study is the study of the processes of transformation" (Ibid.: 99). Accordingly, the Lynds have provided us with the instruments to analyze industrialization, in a moment of great change in factory life and in the life that went on around the factory. Though today there are few communities left that are still in transition from preindustrial economies to industrial ones, the Lynds' analysis could be useful for countries and communities still in the process of industrialization.

Great transformations brought about the conditions that spurred the growth of urban mass society, which, in turn, came to influence the culture of rural areas, until they too were called "urban societies" (Martinelli 1974). Community studies thus help scholars of the social sciences to gather information about certain basic social structures, such as those found at the local and national levels, which, as Stein has said, "cut through the entire national social structure."[23]

Stein emphasized both the peculiarity and the utility of the Lynds' structural, dynamic approach. As opposed to analyses based on "functional" roles that defined only one specific aspect of the individual's participation in society, the community sociologists always consider participation in a whole range of social institutions, each aspect of which influences all the others. The Lynds' analyses of the interconnections existing in the emerging industrial community of Muncie, Indiana, are distinguished precisely by this sense of institutional reciprocity: changes in family consumption could be perceived as central to industry's changing role in promoting those changes, even though the life of the individual and his or her participation in the major institutions of society are always the focus of interest.

In addition—and here a kind of continuity is established between method and technique—

biography can furnish essential data on the changing space of life in keeping with a person's perception of it during the person's life. In turn, changes in individual biography should be studied in a more general context of the changes occurring in the different collective spheres. The "vertical" and "horizontal" dimensions are once again connected: one of the problems central to community studies consists in learning how to coordinate the orders of data.[24]

But was Muncie, as Middletown, America, "typical" during the twenties and thirties? Was it "knowable"? Could information about the interrelations of people there be gathered and transmitted to others? In order to reply to these questions, one must place Muncie within the context of urban America at the time; this will show that Muncie was already an example, not of a small city, but of a real urban center (Caplow 1982). Even at the time of the Lynds it had nearly forty thousand inhabitants, and today its population has almost doubled. Its increase in size made the task of the researcher even more complex.

The Lynds have been widely criticized for several reasons: for simplifying the reality of Muncie by excluding minorities of color in the city and identifying only two social classes there instead of six or more, as Lloyd Warner did; for interviewing the wives instead of the less accessible husbands; and for trusting a very small group of informants and a few sources who they believed represented the reality or spirit of Middletown. Their team of five researchers was certainly inadequate; the study of an urban community should include the application of three paradigms of research: anthropological research, empirical investigation carried out by specialists, and the mastery of analytical and archival documents. Simple calculation suggests that forty researchers would be required to investigate a community of sixty thousand people (Caplow 1982).

THE HISTORY OF MUNCIE

When Robert and Helen Lynd chose Muncie for their study on the religious attitudes of an American community, they had in mind a community that was "knowable" and representative in terms of both history and size.

The first inhabitants of what is today Muncie and Delaware County, Indiana, were the Delaware Indians, who arrived from Ohio in 1770 and established themselves on land belonging to the Miami Indians who had permitted them its use. The Delaware founded several cities along the course of the White River, called by them the *Wa-pi-ha-ni*. One of these cities was four miles from the present courthouse and was called *Buck-on-ge-he-ls-tow*, or "Old Town Hill," because it was the place where the tribal chief lived. Another was "Munsee Town" of the Delaware, which was found within today's city limits; and it was from this Indian village that the present-day city took its name, officially becoming Muncie in 1845.

With the treaty of St. Mary's, Ohio, in 1818, the Delaware Indians ceded their Ohio and Indiana territories to the government of the United States and in 1820 began their migration west toward Kansas and Oklahoma. The territory was then opened officially to white settlement, though there were earlier illegal settlements in the same area. Goldsmith C. Gilbert, born in New York in 1795, is remembered as one of the first colonists of Muncie. He established himself in the northern part of the county and set up a trading post there that was later burned down by a drunken Indian. He was compensated for it by the federal government with a sum of money that was deducted from the Indians' annual income. With 960 dollars, Gilbert acquired "Hackey Reserve" in 1825, an area of 672 acres that became the heart of present-day Muncie. Gilbert constructed two cabins in the clearing that is now Court of Justice Square. He used one as a living space and the other as a trading post.

In April 1827, state law granted Delaware County official existence. In June, the government commissioners gathered at Gilbert's home to choose for the county seat either Muncie or another contestant that had proposed itself insistently, the rapidly expanding community of Granville in the northern part of the county. Tradition has it that the deciding vote in choosing "Muncietown" was very likely the proposal put forward by Gilbert, Jackson, and Brown. These three men proposed to donate about fifty acres of land, part of which would be the location for the courthouse, the rest being sold in lots by the county. The offer was accepted and thus Muncietown became the county seat. Its existence became official.

From that time, the village of Muncietown grew steadily. In 1852, the Indianapolis and Bellefontaine Railroad arrived and in 1854, Muncie was declared a "city." In 1856, it was declared a city with its own government and John Brady was its first mayor.

By 1886, the population of Muncie had reached six thousand, but the real impetus to its growth and its industrial development were given in that year by the discovery of natural gas in Delaware County. Ten years earlier, a squad of workers drilling in search of coal had discovered a gaseous, malodorous substance, whereupon they quickly sealed the drill hole once again. When gas fields were discovered in western Ohio in 1886, the discovery at Eaton was recalled and a certain George Canter put together a company that drilled again and found gas in September 1886. The people of Muncie were enthusiastic about the discovery of this new source of energy, and the drilling of wells there produced the first natural-gas well in November 1886. The gas business had begun, establishing the basis for the future development and industrialization of the city. Muncie's destiny as an industrial city in the heart of a rich agricultural region was now decided. The prospect of an inexhaustible supply of gas encouraged the construction of numerous factories and the city became the "industrious community" of which the pioneers had dreamed, the ideal place for the growth of community spirit in a land rich in natural resources. In 1886, the famous Ball Brothers Company, the main stem of the "X family" entrepreneurs, established itself in Muncie. It later became the Ball Corporation.

During the 1890's several glass and steel manufacturing plants were established in the city, some financed by the Citizen Enterprise Association, which gathered as much as two hundred thousand dollars to finance the new industries. The steel plant included the Midland Steel Company, then part of the U.S. Steel Corporation, and the Iron and Steel Company, better known as "the grasshopper factory" because it was built in some woods that were rife with those insects.

James Boyce, Theodore F. Rose, Joseph A. Goddard, Jacob Henry Wysor, Charles H. Church, and George W. Spilker were all Muncie men who were associated with the industrial and commercial expansion during the thriving gas era. In particular, James Boyce was responsible for the transfer of the Ball factory from Buffalo to Muncie. He met Frank C. Ball on his arrival and took him around in a carriage to show him the possibilities that the area offered. Mr. Ball was president of the business until his death in 1943 at the age of eighty-six.

Meanwhile, the gas was used, misused, and wasted. It was even piped to other areas beyond the western Indiana deposits, the famous "Gas Belt," because it was thought that the reserves would last hundreds of years. But this was not to be: the moment arrived when the gas was exhausted. When it ran out, other big changes took place in Muncie: last-minute efforts were made to conserve the precious natural resource—by the construction of a pumping station to increase gas pressure, for example. Some businesses were transformed into coal-fueled plants that were very costly, and many industries did not survive the dissipation of natural gas. The city had been established as an industrial zone, however, and even the hard times that followed the exhaustion of the natural-gas supply would not change that.

MIDDLETOWN: THE ATYPICAL BEGINNING OF THE RESEARCH

As explained by the Lynds in the very first pages of their text, Muncie was selected as a paradigm of the American way of life because of its history and ambience: its temperate climate; its high growth rate; its lack of distinguishing characteristics; the absence of a college (now central to the life of Muncie/Middletown); its geographic location in the socially desolate prairies; its lack of a significant community of immigrants or other racial minorities; its being industrial, but neither a leader of industry nor a satellite city; and its being the center of community and philanthropic activity for the surrounding territory. In contrast to the approach of the

Chicago School of sociology, Robert and Helen Lynd chose Muncie, as both stated on several occasions over the years, simply because there was nothing extraordinary about it.[25] In fact, the Chicago sociologists during those same years preferred to study cities with a mixed ethnic composition because these were considered to be typical of modern American society. They came to view Chicago as representative of the contradictions resulting from the rapid urbanization taking place in America in the decade between 1920 and 1930, contradictions that also influenced the smaller midwestern cities surrounding Chicago, one of which was chosen by the Lynds as the subject of their research.

The influx of immigration, urban growth, and new forms of industrialization occurring in the first decades of the century in America generated social differences in special interests, ease of mobility, problems of integration, and, as also shown by the Lynds, reinforced individualism as a lifestyle. In the accelerated rhythms of the metropolis, change was spinning out of control and exploding in dissatisfaction, anomie, and conflict, and was destroying old values without creating new ones to take their place. According to Park, only in the long run and together with adequate reforms would these changes have brought about greater liberty and a higher standard of living.[26]

On the whole, the Lynds agreed with the assessments made by these scholars, but when they came to choose a community that could symbolize traditional American virtue and spiritual energy, they chose a "homogenous" city—or so they made it seem. It has been rightly observed that the immediacy of the Lynds' writing at times obscured the structure and objectives of their study as well as its meaning.[27]

The Lynds wanted to examine the cultural changes occurring in an American community between the Victorian era and the mid-1920's. Their choosing a homogenous city was supposed to make it possible for them to observe the changes there in all their transparency and depth. Thus, the "nonethnic," unmixed character of the population was essential: the ideal community had to be composed predominantly of people of white, Anglo-Saxon, Protestant origin—born in Muncie, having absorbed both "Yankee" and Southern culture—and had to be located in the Midwest. One further simplification of concept and method was the premise of the existence of only two classes: the "business" class and the "working" class, or rather, in American sociological language, white collar and blue collar. The Lynds themselves admitted that these categories were simplified and imprecise, but claimed that they were appropriate for enlarging the scope of their research, making it possible to grasp the social phenomenology of this city of thirty-five thousand inhabitants.

*

The Lynds arrived in Muncie in January 1924. Even today the irony of their situation is striking: two young researchers whose combined age was under fifty, and who had no specific training or practical sociological experience, established themselves in a city that had been chosen at the last moment for a religious study that was financed by John D. Rockefeller, a man who had lost his religious convictions some time earlier, if he ever had any. Yet it was Rockefeller who gave impetus to the Middletown project, even though it underwent various mutations en route to its unintended sociological destination.

A mining center in Colorado, Cripple Creek, was the setting for a bloody workers' struggle in 1903–1904. Shocked by what came to be called the Cripple Creek Massacre, Rockefeller began to consider the best way to attenuate the hostility between business owners and workers. Religion was one potential means; thus, in the two years from 1919 to 1920, he financed the Interchurch World movement, through which he and his colleagues sought to create the church of the future, in which pragmatic, YMCA-style Christianity and the social services would foster class harmony.

The movement was unsuccessful, however, bringing Rockefeller both disappointment and economic loss. Raymond Fosdik helped dissolve Interchurch World and its funds were transferred to a new body, the Committee for Religious and Social Investigation. In 1923, this committee became the Institute for Social and Religious Research and commissioned new studies with the same objective of Interchurch World: to unify the Protestant churches into one vast network of social services. In its thirteen years of existence (1921–34), the Institute was able to complete forty-eight research projects and to publish seventy-eight books, including the volumes by H. Paul Douglas, a noted pastor in Iowa. Douglas joined the Institute in 1921 and wrote twelve books based on the research he carried out in Iowa, namely, *St. Louis Church Survey* (1924), *A Suburban Trend* (1925), *The Springfield Church Survey* (1926), *A Thousand City Churches* (1926), *The Church in the Changing City* (1927), and *How to Study the City Church* (1928).

Finally, the directors of the Institute concluded that the organization should do more than just research churches and communities, since these investigations had been carried out too quickly and had been notably quantitative in nature. It was decided, therefore, to dedicate more attention to the "Small City Study" that would analyze all of the religious practices observed in an industrial center. The study would go beyond the usual investigation into the religious convictions of the population and the capacity of religious bodies to respond to the requirements of the community: it would highlight the latent psychological factors of the community more than the external, observable, measurable components.

Initially, the Institute chose the sociologist Louis Bailey, of Northwestern University, as director of the study, but he was soon removed because, it was said, although he was diligent he was not a good observer of detail and did not have the capacity for in-depth analysis. Bailey had already begun to consider which cities to investigate, beginning with those suggested by the Institute: Springfield, Massachusetts, and Johnstown, Pennsylvania. Later, he presented a list that included South Bend, Indiana; Flint, Lansing, Jackson, Kalamazoo, Muskegan, Pontiac, and Port Huron, Michigan; Canton, Steubenville, and Warren, Ohio; Racine and Kenasha, Wisconsin; and Rockford, Illinois. The Institute accepted the substitution and reduced the list to five: South Bend, Steubenville, Kenasha, Rockford, and Jackson. The Committee had established the requisite that the city would include a high percentage of foreign residents. But Bailey had employed other criteria: the chosen city must have had a growth rate of at least 35 percent in the decade preceding the research; had to have a county seat in midwestern America; and had to include representatives of all the major religions of the United States.

The man who took Bailey's place was not a sociologist; he was the young graduate from Union Theological Seminary, Robert S. Lynd. Born in 1892 in New Albany, Indiana (on the border of Kentucky), Lynd was the descendant of an old American family of pioneers. His great-grandfather had been a Presbyterian pastor who had attended Princeton University, but, after him, his descendants had fallen on hard times. Lynd's grandfather was a doctor in Cincinnati, but became an alcoholic, forcing his father to drop out of high school to work in a bank. He was transferred to New York, where by dint of hard work and talent he became president of Manufacturer's Trust Bank.

Lynd went to school in Indiana and graduated from Princeton in 1914.[28] His wife, Helen, recalled that the years at Princeton were difficult for Robert as his family resources were much more modest than those of his fellow students. He then became an editor for *Publisher's Weekly* and subsequently held various posts in the field of editing and publishing. In 1918, he enrolled in the army: his military experiences changed the objectives of his career. While ill in the hospital, he began taking care of other soldiers and decided then that his true vocation was social service.

After his discharge, he enrolled in Union Theological Seminary and, while there, attended two social-science courses at Columbia University. These courses were taught by two people who would profoundly influence the social convictions of the young Robert: John Dewey, the great

American philosopher, and Wesley Mitchell, a well-known economist. Lynd found Mitchell's *The Backward Art of Spending* (1912)—an essay influenced by the work of Veblen on human irrationality and conspicuous consumption created by new wealth—particularly congenial.

While he was attending Union Theological Seminary, Lynd had another meaningful experience, destined to change his life. In the spring of 1921, he applied for summer work with the Presbyterian Board of Home Missions. The missionary committee gave him the choice of preaching in an established church in rural Indiana or establishing a new church in an oil camp in Wyoming. The young Robert chose the latter and moved to Elk Basin. Once there, however, he assumed responsibilities well beyond those originally assigned to him. In addition to organizing Bible study groups, which was part of his original assignment, he taught Sunday school, formed squads of young Boy Scouts, and worked as a laborer in the oil camp. He described these experiences in three articles: the first, "But Why Preach?," published anonymously in *Harper's* in 1921; the second, "Crude-Oil Religion," with the author identified, in *Harper's*, 1922; and the third, "Done in Oil," which appeared in *Survey* in 1922.

According to Fox (1983), "Crude-Oil Religion" narrated Lynd's experiences as pastor and worker in Wyoming and presaged the Middletown study. At Elk Basin, in fact, Lynd had his first vision of the *Gemeinschaft*, the integrated, supportive community for which he would always yearn. When he began his research in Muncie in 1924, this longing for a solid community would be transposed by Lynd onto his image of what Muncie was like in 1890. The article "Done in Oil" was a scourging attack on Standard Oil of Indiana and on John Rockefeller Jr., inspired by the harsh conditions of life in the oil camps. Lynd's son, the historian and lawyer Staughton Lynd, has noted that there was little space dedicated to religion and much to political criticism in the controversial article. In tone and substance, the article described a community that resembled Muncie during the twenties—at least in terms of antagonistic power relationships. One student of Lynd concluded that *Middletown* was not so much the comparison of two distinct periods in the development of a city in the Midwest as the description of two personal struggles in Lynd's life (Fox 1983).

Though Rockefeller did not appreciate the depiction in "Done in Oil," and even attempted to block the book's publication, he did not harbor resentment for the young author and even chose Lynd as the new director of the Small City Study. He was supported in this choice by Raymond Fosdick, one of his legal advisors.

In the meantime, three days after his return from Elk Basin, Robert married Helen Merrell, who was destined to be not only his lifetime companion but also the coauthor of the *Middletown* volumes. The two young people had met by chance during a climb of Mount Washington (both would remain passionate mountain climbers). After their meeting, Helen told Lynd about her enthusiasm for a book she was reading, *The Theory of the Leisure Class*, by Thorstein Veblen.[29] Robert was quite taken by this girl who had such unexpected taste in books, and the two continued to see one another while Robert was at the seminary and Helen was teaching in a girls' school. After their marriage, they lived with Robert's parents in New York City while Helen completed her master's degree at Columbia. Like her husband, Helen was not trained as a sociologist, but as a humanist.[30]

When Lynd took over the Small City Study in 1923, he was permitted to choose the community that he intended to examine. He chose South Bend, Indiana, but abandoned that plan in November when he was forced to admit that the city was too big and had too much ethnic variety. He then compiled a short list of other possible cities: Decatur, Illinois, as well as Kokomo and Muncie, Indiana. Finally, he chose Muncie.

By choosing Muncie, Lynd had annulled Bailey's original criterion of a wide ethnic base. No city in the Midwest at the time (Jensen 1979), with twenty-five thousand inhabitants, had a percentage of population of old local stock greater than Muncie. Lynd described his community as "the most representative possible in contemporary America."

The testimony of the Lynds[31] makes clear that the small group of researchers found themselves ensnared at first in a perplexing tangle of complications. They found their way through it by means of classical trial-and-error methods and by using as many and various sources as possible. When the results were analyzed and put in book form, the Lynds then encountered great difficulty in having it published. Raymond Fosdick, who had originally supported the research, did not like the finished product and opposed its publication: the book was too much "a thesis" and its range of ideas, theories, and arguments was baffling. Facts and values were confused and fragments of reality were dispersed in a prolix, tedious narration, the scientific credibility of which was doubtful. As Helen later recalled, the original supporters thought it uninteresting and, worse, irreligious. It was finally published, not by the Institute, but by Harcourt and Brace, after Alfred Harcourt had read it. It was an immediate success, featured in book reviews in the *Herald Tribune* and the *New York Times*, including the first page of the *Times Book Review*. Helen remembered that the window at Brentano's was filled with copies of *Middletown*. And its success was lasting: *Middletown* is one of the few volumes of social science written in twentieth-century United States that has never gone out of print.

Much of the success of *Middletown* was due to the combination of its literary style, its "narrative" power (Wilson 1974), and its effective use of irony as a literary device that enabled the authors to recount the experi-

ences of the people of Middletown while at the same time critically com-
menting on them. According to Stein, the Lynds compare favorably with
at least two other highly competent American social critics of the time:
the sharp-cutting irony of Sinclair Lewis and the intensity of Veblen.

Along with a distinctive literary style, the book was successful because
of what it contained. Indeed, the Lynds had much to say in *Middletown*.
The book is full of the details of everyday life: what time the members of
the two social classes got up in the morning; who made his or her own
bread and who bought it; who owned an automobile and what they used
it for; who went to the cinema; how the wash was done; what was taught
in the schools; who went to church; how many people got married and
how many got divorced; and what the values were of the different social
classes. In addition, the Lynds analyzed the changes occurring in the city
itself between 1890 and 1920.

From a harmonious community composed mostly of craftsmen,
Muncie had become a divided city of restless factory workers toiling to
survive in a heartless, industrial system. The "freedom" to buy consumer
goods contrasted with social immobility. Real social ascent was permitted
to the business class only, but especially to the "power elite."

Meanwhile, the two young authors of Middletown had assumed new
responsibilities in their careers even before the publishing of their book.
In 1928, Helen Lynd began her long career as a teacher at Sarah Lawrence
College in Bronxville, New York, while Robert became secretary of the
Social Sciences Research Council. After the success of *Middletown*, he received two teaching offers: one at the University of Michigan and the
other at Columbia University. He chose Columbia and began to teach
there in 1931, after finishing his Ph.D. on Middletown. (Helen recalled
later that in order to make the book suitable for his doctoral dissertation,
they had to "mark with a blue pen" those parts of the book that had been
written by Robert, in order to distinguish them from those written by
Helen.[32])

Under President Roosevelt, who named Robert a member of the Consumer's Advisory Board, Lynd addressed his scientific interests to consumer consumption and the quality of life after the Depression. In particular, he developed two research projects: one about the impact of the great
crisis on 150 "white" families in Manhattan, and the second about 200
well-to-do families in Montclair, New Jersey. Instead of completing the
two works of research, however, he returned to Middletown.

THE CHOICE OF METHOD

In order to understand the community and then render it comprehensible
to others, the Lynds established certain simple methodological priorities

along with some precautionary rules. They were well aware of how complex an entire microcosm would be to investigate, and they intended to approach the study as if they had dropped down into Muncie like two "visitors from another world" (though Robert was born in the state). At the beginning, they did not know where this approach would take them.

The Lynds adopted the classification system developed by the English social anthropologists Rivers and Wissler,[33] which assumes that certain activities are common to all human beings in all types of society. In the words of the Lynds:

Whether in an Arunta village in Central Australia or in our own seemingly intricate institutional life of corporations, dividends, coming-out parties, prayer meetings, freshmen, and Congress, human behavior appears to consist in variations upon a few major lines of activity: getting the material necessities for food, clothing, shelter; mating; initiating the young into the group habits of thought and behavior; and so on. This study, accordingly, proceeds on the assumption that all the things people do in this American city may be viewed as falling under one or another of the following six main-trunk activities:

> Getting a living.
> Making a home.
> Training the young.
> Using leisure in various forms of play, art, and so on.
> Engaging in religious practices.
> Engaging in community activities.[34]

The Lynds gathered data in each category and then analyzed them by using Wissler's paradigm of universal cultural viewpoints and Radcliffe-Brown's system of decodifying the meaning of social customs. Gradually, the Lynds found their method of proceeding via a system of trial and error. They adopted the year 1890 as their reference point in order to place their research in proper historical perspective: "The following pages aim to present a dynamic, functional study of the contemporary life of this specific American community in the light of the trends of changing behavior observable in it during the last thirty-five years."[35]

After several attempts to identify the different social groups in the city, they decided that "the differentiation which most adequately represented the facts was that into business class and working class."[36] Their data was fundamentally qualitative and included what we call today "participatory observation," which they defined as "participation in the local life." It also included examination of documentary material, compilation of statistics, interviews, and questionnaires. Concerning their method of observation, they wrote, "In reporting meetings attended, as in individual interviews or casual conversations, the method followed was to take such inconspicuous notes as were possible in the course of the meeting, service, or interview and then immediately afterward to write them up in detail according to the standardized form adopted."[37]

Statistical data, archives, as well as city, county, and school documents were used as sources. In addition, they read the two daily newspapers in detail for the years 1890 and 1891. During the year and a half of research, they read and clipped out articles from two republican dailies and the democratic weekly, and did the same, in less detail, for the following year. Records of different organizations, histories of the state, the county, and the city, books on the economic boom, and citizen investigations were examined. Finally, regarding more complex, qualitative aspects,

Two unusually detailed diaries, one of a leading merchant and prominent Protestant churchman and one of a young Catholic baker, were read for the years 1886 to 1900. These and various other diaries and "scrap books" of clippings, programs, letters, club papers, etc., when coupled with the memories of older citizens, helped to supply for the earlier period a partial equivalent for the informal person-to-person contacts and folk-talk of today.[38]

Statistical data covered salary, continuity of employment, job-related accidents, distance between home and work, social promotion, belongings, charitable contributions, attendance of clubs and church, the circulation of library books and periodicals, attendance at the cinema, ownership and the use of the automobile, and so on. In addition, the interviews "varied all the way from the most casual conversation with street-car conductors, janitors, barbers, or chance associates at luncheon or club meeting to carefully planned interviews."[39] Techniques and tools varied as research progressed, from the famous "interviews" (124 in all) of working-class and (40) well-to-do wives, to the questionnaires administered to the school population two to three years before the research. A total of 700 to 800 students were interviewed about school, and another 550 were interviewed about public matters (with true-or-false responses).

Of the six areas of life singled out for examination, the one that received the most attention was "getting a living," which was also the area that provided the most information about and the best explanation of life in Middletown. All of the other activities depended on "getting a living" and on the fundamental dichotomy of class that it implied.

What Life Was Like in Middletown

The Lynds' sponsors wanted a study on religious life in America, but they rightly understood that religion was best comprehended when placed in a wider context. The Lynds' chosen method (in fact, more declared than re-

alized)—lighting upon Muncie as if they were investigating a newly discovered primitive community—was consistent with this basic approach.

Inspired by the idea of "the Americanization of Marx,"[40] the Lynds en-
riched their research with that fruitful empirical dimension, which, in the
last analysis, characterized their contribution to sociology. They established from the outset that work was the central activity of the inhabitants
of Middletown.

A stranger unfamiliar with the ways of Middletown, dropped down into the city,
as was the field staff in January, 1924, would be a lonely person. He would find
people intently engaged day after day in some largely routinized, specialized occupation. Only the infants, the totteringly old, and a fringe of women would
seem to be available to answer his endless questions.

In a word—

> 43 people out of every 100 in Middletown are primarily
> occupied with getting the living of the entire group.
> 23 of every 100 are engaged in making the homes of the
> bulk of the city.
> 19 of every 100 are receiving day after day the training
> required of the young.
> 15 of every 100, the remainder, are chiefly those under six
> years, and the very old.[41]

By emphasizing the centrality of work and "getting a living," the Lynds
made Middletown a kind of dramatization of the mental world of Marx.
Through the everyday language of the typical midwestern American, the
authors wanted to demonstrate how capitalistic values distorted the various aspects of life in an average American city.

THE DILEMMA OF CLASS

As soon as work was divided into two principal types of activity, the
Lynds adopted a model for stratifying the two classes. In their scheme,
which varied to some extent during the course of the research, the different occupations were subdivided into two groups, one for the working
class and the other for the business class. In the Lynds' words:

Members of the first group, by and large, address their activities in getting their
living primarily to *things*, utilizing material tools in the making of things and the
performance of services, while the members of the second group address their activities predominantly to *people* in the seeing or promotion of things, services, and
ideas. . . . If the Federal Census distribution of those gainfully employed in
Middletown in 1920 is reclassified according to this grouping we find that there
are two and one-half times as many in the working class as in the business class—
seventy-one in each 100 as against twenty-nine.[42]

Within the sphere of the four hundred types of work in Middletown that included both classes, the possible distinctions were many. For example 4 percent of the business class, which constituted 29 percent of the working population, consisted of a group that used sophisticated tools—architects, surgeons, pharmacists, and so forth. Although these individuals dedicated their working activity more to things than to people, they could not be included in the working class because all their other activities identified them with the business class.

The two young authors were well aware of the fact that within the two social groups there existed an infinity of gradations: on one hand, from the simple unskilled worker to the foreman, and on the other, from the simple employee to the owner of a business or a professional. Moreover, they admitted that the objective of their study was not to trace a detailed diagram by which the multitude of groupings observable in Middletown could be deciphered in detail, but rather to characterize the meaningful features of its social morphology.

This choice was neither simple nor painless; it was not so much the result of long theoretical reflection as it was dictated by the empirical data themselves. The researchers reconstructed their course of action in an especially important note in the text:

Careful consideration was given to the applicability for the purposes of this study of the conventional tripartite division into Lower Class, Middle Class, and Upper Class. This was rejected, however, for the following reasons: (1) Since the dominance of the local getting-a-living activities impresses upon the group a pattern of social stratification based primarily upon vocational activity, it seemed advisable to utilize terms that hold this vocational cleavage to the fore. (2) In so far as the traditional three-fold classification might be applied to Middletown today, the city would have to be regarded as having only a lower and a middle class; eight or nine households might conceivably be considered as an upper class, but these families are not a group apart but are merged in the life of the mass of businessfolk.[43]

Regarding the criteria for distinguishing the two groups, the Lynds were aware that there are other terms of social differentiation based on different professional activities: "people who address their activities to things and people who address their activities to persons; those who work with their hands and those who work with their tongues; those who make things and those who sell or promote things and ideas; those who use material tools and those who use various non-material institutional devices."[44]

The first inkling of an upper business class *within* the business class would receive attention and confirmation in *Middletown in Transition*; the dominant role played by the X family would emerge within that very small group.

Beyond the fissures in the social fabric of Middletown, the Lynds were also very sensitive to the rhythms, actions, and habits of life in the city. They made allowances for various age groups, for gender, and for individual characteristics. In general, on the basis of empirical observation it could be affirmed that "the working class today employs the habits of the business class of roughly a generation ago; if it were possible to differentiate clearly the gradations by which each of these two major groups shades into the other, it might appear that many changes are slowly filtered down through various intermediate groups."[45] With this last notation, the way was open to other possible interpretations of the "social destiny" of the groups in Middletown. It should be mentioned here, in anticipation of subjects covered in the last chapter, that the past decade has witnessed a certain process of increasing egalitarianism (at least in terms of lifestyle) in the city.

It appears clear, then, that the Lynds do not use the Marxian category of salaried work as the fundamental characteristic of differentiation between the two groups, but use instead the feature of control as the basic element in their analysis of class as well as in their observation of such institutions as schools, churches, health care, participation in public activities, and free time. The primacy of "getting a living" makes the workplace the most important institution in Middletown. The instruments of domination are extended to ensure that control of the workplace remains in the hands of the business people rather than in those of the workers. "Getting a living" comprises, at the same time, many areas of society. Thus, in any assessment of the business class's mechanism of control of the means of production, it is necessary to take into account the participants in these other institutional areas.

On the basis of this substantial class opposition:

The mere fact of being born upon one or the other side of the watershed roughly formed by these two groups is the most significant single cultural factor tending to influence what one does all day long throughout one's life; whom one marries; when one gets up in the morning; whether one belongs to the Holy Roller or Presbyterian church; or drives a Ford or a Buick; whether or not one's daughter makes the desirable high school Violet Club; or one's wife meets with the Sew We Do Club or with the Art Students' League; whether one belongs to the Odd Fellows or to the Masonic Shrine; whether one sits about evenings with one's necktie off; and so on indefinitely throughout the daily comings and goings of Middletown man, woman, or child.[46]

The determining factor of class extended to all spheres of life: from income to lifestyle, in different social opportunities, in economic interests and in the distribution of power, and especially, in social power and politics. As a well-known Italian scholar has noted, social and political power "was in the hands of business, or rather of its internal capitalistic nucleus, which was most interested in defending its direct economic interests and more generally, its domain (witness the struggle against the organized workers' movement and against its dissent)."[47]

The activities of the Ku Klux Klan, which established itself in Muncie just before the Lynds' research, showed the upper class's capacity for political action. Nonetheless, the authors do not dedicate much space in the text to the Klan's turbulent affairs in either Muncie or elsewhere in Indiana in the first half of the twenties, even though their documentation on the subject was vast. Pages and pages of notes, never used, can still be found in the manuscripts in the archives of the Muncie Library, where I had a chance to see them among the Lynd Papers. The Lynds devoted only a few phrases in the text to the movement, aside from reference to it as part of the "negative myth" of America. They portray in this regard:

Coming upon Middletown like a tornado . . . the Ku Klux Klan has emphasized, during its brief career in Middletown, potential factors of disintegration. Brought to town originally, it is said, by a few of the city's leading business men as a vigilance committee to hold an invisible whip over the corrupt Democratic political administration and generally "to clean up the town," its ranks were quickly thrown open under a professional organizer, and by 1923 some 3,500 of the local citizens are said to have joined. As the organization developed, the business men withdrew, and the Klan became largely a working class movement. Thus relieved of the issue that prompted its original entry into Middletown, the Klan, lacking a local issue, took over from the larger national organization a militant Protestantism with which it set about dividing the city; the racial issue, though secondary, was hardly less ardently proclaimed. . . . The high tide of bitterness was reached in 1923, and by 1925 the energy was mainly spent and the Klan disappeared as a local power, leaving in its wake wide areas of local bitterness.[48]

Yet another fundamental point of difference between the two antagonistic social groups was class consciousness. The "great transformation" occurring in Middletown, as in many other American cities of the time, resulted in the loss of the spirit of community and a weakening of class consciousness, which even before was never very strong. This dissolution of worker identity (both on the job and in one's personal life) did not stop with the crises of capitalism, but actually got worse, as Lynd attempted to demonstrate in his second research. Class consciousness seemed to become another privilege of the business class, which, being on the ascendant, had to keep the material and symbolic elements of its own identity under control. Social mobility—or immobility—thus became a fundamental indicator for discriminating between the two classes. This, however, was rooted in another American myth that the Lynds' research was meant to denounce: the idea that success was available for everyone, and that poverty is a result of individual failure. The problem was clearly formulated as follows:

The belief that the gifted, inventive, motivated American worker held in his rag-bag of tricks the lucky entrepreneur's magic wand was part of the official ideal for some time, and was earnestly preached and defended by business. It was enhanced as well for a long while by the objectives and exceptional opportunities offered by the American frontier, by the America of the greatest economic development in history. But in truth, in the new phase of national organization and capitalistic development, great mobility was increasingly difficult; and the Lynds were among the very first to attack the sacred myth and the discouraging data of logical-empirical research on mobility from one generation to another.[49]

More specifically, Cavalli deduces three steps of mobility from the Lynds' analysis. According to the Italian scholar, the first step

is the mobility from worker to management, which is certainly missing in Middletown in connection with the objective lack of management positions. The second is mobility to positions in the business class, which have become very scarce during the phase of capitalistic development, positions that require superior technical or bureaucratic skills and, therefore, further training. The third and last, central to the myth of mobility, is the step to independent entrepreneur. But this step had become very difficult for the average worker because, in order to set up a business, an increasingly higher sum of capital was required, and it was ever more difficult for a working-class person to obtain credit. In conclusion, mobility from working to business class from one generation to another was small. . . . The promise of intergenerational mobility remains for those sons and daughters who have received higher education, but the Lynds cast no encouraging light on this alternative.[50]

Thus, the reader recognizes in the Lynds' Middletown a process of pro-gressive co-optation of working-class prerogatives by the business class. Above all, the weak resistance of the working class to the intimidation of the upper class was rooted in habits ingrained from generations of life on the farm in a cultural hinterland with an ideology of self-sufficiency, independence, and individualism. The ideology of consumption, continu-ally reinforced through the rituals of daily life, provided another powerful endorsement of the behavior of the business class.

Alienation thus diminished the stature of the producer-citizens of Middletown: people worked but they did not see the finished product of their own labor. The Lynds gave an example:

The annual output of a single plant, employing a thousand of the city's total of 17,000 who get its living, aggregates $12,000,000; everything this plant makes is promptly shipped away, and perhaps one-tenth of 1 per cent. of it ever returns as a few obscure parts hidden in some of the automobiles Middletown drives.

And this gap between the things the people do to get a living and the actual needs of living is widening."[51]

DAILY LIFE IN MIDDLETOWN

As already noted, the class one belonged to pervaded every aspect of life in Middletown, even the time at which one got up in the morning (working-class people had to get up early, while businessmen could sleep longer). Here, then, were the small but concrete indicators of the diverse and divided quality of life in the city.

Fathers belonging to the working class had already left for work when their children came down for breakfast. Thus, the working class was unable to follow the advice of an editorial in a local newspaper to reinforce family life by interacting with children at breakfast. Class also influenced the choice of places where people lived, how they voted, and even their opinions about daylight saving time: the workers were opposed to it while businessmen were in favor. The former wanted more hours of daylight while the latter desired more time for golf.

The first volume on Middletown analyzes daily life in the city according to six anthropological categories, as follows:

1. Getting a living. The class to which one belonged determined the number of hours of work and whether the person worked at night. The working class worked more hours than the business class and often had to work the night shift, which meant that they participated less in family life and in community activities. The working class, in addition, was continually threatened by unemployment.

2. Making a home. The instability of jobs in industry was linked to the abandonment of old habits of living near the work place and the creation of small, integrated communities of working-class people. The breakup of the working-class neighborhood counterbalanced the departure from the city center and consequent increase in space for the business class. Already by the twenties, the well-to-do class was constructing its neighborhoods distant from the rest of the city, where it was impossible for members of the working class to come.

3. Training the young. The mothers belonging to the well-to-do classes were privileged to be able to dedicate themselves to raising and educating their children, whereas the pressure of outside work or hard work in the home did not allow wives and mothers from the working classes to do the same.

4. The use of leisure time. For people of the working class, gatherings with friends took place in the neighborhood, while for the well-to-do class, the element of "propinquity" was not at all determining, and particularly so for the younger generation. Choral music, once cultivated and shared by all citizens of Middletown, by 1925 seemed

far less common than a generation ago. Serenading is a thing of the past. Chorus choirs are disappearing in the churches most frequented by the business class. There is today no chorus of business class men. In the city of today, nearly three and one-half times as large as that of 1890, there are only two adult musical societies in which the earlier tradition survives, as over against four in 1890. The first is a chorus of working class men. This, together with the chorus choirs in working class churches and the frequent appearance of songs and recitations in the 1890 manner in the "socials" of the churches, suggests the relatively greater place of singing and playing in the play life of working class adults. It suggests, too, the tendency noted elsewhere for many of the workers' habits to lag roughly a generation behind those of the business class.[52]

5. Religion. Members of the working class were more fervent in their religious convictions than those of the well-to-do class, in which the Lynds noted a decline in certain beliefs—the belief in the existence of heaven and hell, for example. In general, while religion was still important for workers, it became increasingly formalistic for the business class.

6. Community activities. Once again comparing 1890 with the twenties, the Lynds found that worker cohesion diminished with the growth of various associations such as the Chamber of Commerce, the Rotary Club, and the Publicity Club.

From this brief picture, the general decline of the "quality of life" emerged. The examination of daily life in the city was a crucial factor in the great depiction of Middletown. Despite the unmistakable changes that have occurred since the book was written, even today's reader will find the complex picture of daily life in Muncie more or less familiar, like a remarkable déjà vu.

The first volume on Middletown shows the Lynds' radical views on and criticism of the decline of traditional American values. They identified two especially problematic areas: nonworking, or leisure, time, and independent associations, which had been extolled by de Tocqueville as one of the best products of American democracy. But we shall return later to this point, so central for understanding the past and present of "American" life in Middletown.

The two authors' analysis showed that, little by little, independent associations were becoming more formalized, paralleling religious practice. The latter, emptied of meaning, carried out the legitimizing function of providing reassurance and psychological support in a situation of class antagonism.

The Lynds' discussion of leisure is a good example of the approach used for their analysis of Middletown. The progressive decrease in recreational practices was linked to the process of social and environmental degradation caused by senseless industrialization. The following description by the

Lynds is pertinent: "A small river wanders through Middletown, and in 1890 when timber still stood on its banks, White River was a pleasant stream for picnics, fishing, and boating, but it has shrunk today to a creek, discolored by industrial chemicals and malodorous with the city's sewage."[53]

Already at the time of the Lynds, the people of Middletown had at their disposal a much greater quantity of material things than the preceding generation. The Lynds affirm that "the lessening of the number of hours spent daily in getting a living and in home-making and the almost universal habit of the Saturday half-holiday combine with these new possibilities for spending an extra hour to make leisure a more generally expected part of every day rather than a more sporadic, semi-occasional event."[54]

With the increase of nonworking time consequent to the general improvement in the standard of living, a space for leisure time seemed to open up but immediately close again because of the bad use that people made of it: another of the cultural contradictions that distorted "American values."

One favorite recreational activity of the citizens of Middletown was public speaking. Whether in the form of conferences, sermons, or gossip, and regardless of the content, eloquence had always been much admired by the inhabitants of Middletown—and even more so in 1925. But even this activity underwent a transformation of content: the speeches in public were shorter, the orators were no longer interrupted but were listened to passively, and above all, speech became devoid of real content. People no longer went to conferences on specific (if often abstruse) themes, such as "Nicknames of Great Americans," "Milton as an Educator," or "The Uses of Ugliness"; nor did they attend the moral or religious lectures. The Lynds noted the process of "secularization" of conferences and conference members: that more substantial type of meeting was substituted more and more with brief talks by club members on specific themes and for specialized groups. Specialization seemed to kill the simple spontaneity of the citizens of yesterday.

Reading also occupied an important place in the use of free time, and quantitatively the situation appeared very much improved relative to 1890. In 1925, there were about forty thousand books in the libraries of Middletown, fifteen times the number in 1890. But the quality of the reading was never particularly high and could be subdivided into two kinds: manuals (from "how to raise babies" to cookbooks) and escapist narratives. In fact, 83 percent of all the books borrowed from the library by the inhabitants of Middletown were low-grade fiction. Essays on the whole were nonexistent; likewise, music, poetry, and other artistic forms. Above all, during the nineties spontaneous singing had been characteristic of every meeting. A young baker's diary, one of the exquisitely "qualitative" sources used by the Lynds, relates the wide diffusion of music of every sort, from rowdy nocturnal bantering to romantic serenades: "Yesterday ——'s birthday, so he set up cigars and a keg at the union meeting. After the meeting we played cards and sang till eleven."[55]

Most of the "good" leisure activities of Middletown, from visits with neighbors to trade-union events, were pushed aside by the new, less spontaneous, and more organized activities, such as societies, clubs, and associations. The connection to the past was lost through modern inventions that promoted new ways of using free time: the automobile, the cinema, and the radio. But even here the disadvantages outweighed the advantages. With the increased mobility provided by the automobile, the young were invited to such sexual license that one local judge from the juvenile court commented that it constituted "a brothel on wheels." The cinema asserted contradictory messages: from films that were too edifying (even in the opinion of the baker who wrote the diary), to those that were purely for escape and lacking in meaning—with dubious influence on the city's young people. Even the radio had an ambivalent function: on one hand it broadened cultural horizons and served as an adhesive for family life, on the other, "it will at the same time operate, with national advertising, syndicated newspapers, and other means of large-scale diffusion, as yet another means of standardizing many of Middletown's habits."[56]

The authors portray the individual citizen of Middletown as one isolated in his own sphere of activity, paradoxically subjected to a greater isolation than that of the past. Is this not, perhaps, the destiny of everyone in a "mass society"?

For a Cultural Renewal

As seen from this brief summary, leisure in Middletown tended to be differentiated by the class divide that marked the whole of life in the city. The "eclipse of the community" muddled the progress toward a better form of human society, resulting instead in the unraveling of the social fabric: new contradictions and a fall into dispersion and isolation, with the ultimate risk of total anonymity (Durkheim [1902] 1966).

Through the Lynds' portrayal of Middletown, one can see how the material developments in capitalistic American society during those years—accelerated by technological advances—were not balanced by an evolution within nonmaterial culture. The craving for new consumer goods seemed to exclude unselfish, more sophisticated ways of relating to others. Human relationships were emptied of substance, reduced to associations of mutual interest, ease, or habit. In addition, an indolent acquiescence

rendered radical dissent unlikely; the familiar conflict of class and of economic interests faded into a general malcontent. In the process, the vi-
cious cycle of alienation was perpetuated and denounced by the Lynds.[57]

Despite their initial declarations of "neutrality," the young authors early
on manifested youthful ardor and a critical spirit. The broken promises
and the false expectations of life in Muncie tested their minds and hearts
as radicals. The Lynds examined the problems of social change, not only in
linear terms of cultural lag; they strongly doubted whether America would
ever be able to construct a "human" society without reworking its very
foundations.

In relation to the dynamism of the "good years"—and regardless of
traditionalist nostalgia—the process of change had taken a turn for the
worse; it had assumed a sluggish, lackluster quality. The Lynds' view of
change, therefore, was twofold: it looked back to what had happened in
the past and it looked forward to what should happen in the future. The
present was veiled, but the future still held the hope (the utopia?) for a
better world that would require work, however, for its renewal.

With lucidity and interpretative richness, the Lynds' research into an
American "world" enabled them to affirm "the possible utility of a
deeper-cutting procedure that would involve a reexamination of the institutions themselves."[58]

And so closes the first book on Middletown.

CHAPTER 3

Middletown II: What Transition?

Social Motivations and Personal Intentions: New Research

Despite a certain feeling of déjà vu, Robert Lynd returned to Middletown to study the effects of the Depression, choosing that city, of course, because he knew it so well. Even though the criterion of "typicalness" was no longer the issue, it was clear that Middletown in the second half of the 1930's constituted a sort of living laboratory for common problems, and for pragmatic solutions projected over a long period of time—all of which was especially dear to Robert, a man of Roosevelt's New Deal.

The second book described the changes in the different spheres of life in Middletown, but the principal change was the one that had occurred within the author himself (Schutz 1971). His life had not "changed" in its basic direction, in the sense that over that decade he had maintained his ideas, enthusiasm, and commitment, still neither embittered nor disillusioned. The success of the first research had transformed him from an unknown, unspecialized researcher to an authority in the field of sociology and a noted professor at Columbia University. He was a respected intellectual, the personal friend of Robert Merton and other already well-known sociologists of the day (or others who would become so), but something in Lynd's attitude had changed: he now tended to take things more at face value, attributing new meanings and emphasizing different aspects of what he observed.

In *Middletown in Transition*, however, he would continue to express the critical vigor and the appetite for "doing" that were among Lynd's distinctive personality traits and that determined his place in the history of sociology. The very style of the book is both forceful and unconventional; it breaks through the bounds of the usual "replication" study, and exposes to the point of denouncing the structural (rather than the cultural) contradictions of one particular phase of capitalism.[1] This is one of the miracles of both of the Lynds' Middletown studies: they not only make good reading, even today, but they are as engaging as a story told by a close, trusted friend.[2]

Controversial and innovative ideas animated the forty-year-old Robert in his revisitation of Middletown. This time he returned without his wife, Helen, who was kept in New York by other familial and professional responsibilities; and his sponsor was no longer the institute financed by John Rockefeller, but his editor, who wanted a second best-seller, a "sequel" to *Middletown*. This new sponsor, however, did not have much money available, and therefore Lynd could neither take on many assistants nor stay in the city very long.

During preparation for the new research, Lynd invited the people of Middletown—and they responded to his invitation—to criticize the city and to furnish information, new ideas, and suggestions about their city and themselves. Marked, moreover, by the spiritual odyssey of the past ten years, he had modified his opinions about what the Middletown experience meant. The five years he had spent under President Roosevelt, researching various aspects of economic consumption, had shown him that the average American had lost his or her rational judgment under the influence of advertising. As an advocate of the New Deal, he even asked for more governmental protection for the population against advertising campaigns. It was that very element of irrationality, of inadequate response in a profoundly crisis-ridden situation, that Lynd would discover in the average Middletown citizen and in his or her unpardonable "propensity for consumption." This was only one of the many problems that motivated Robert to try his hand at a second effort in the field of research. Basically, he had just two hypotheses left: that the city was altogether different than it was before, or that Middletown had not changed much at all because of the "retarding countercurrent of custom."[3]

With these crucial questions in mind, the research group got off the train in Muncie at the beginning of June 1935: the possibility that the responses to their questions would provide indications about the future of the whole of American culture gave them a serious, but excited, air.

CHANGE IN SUBJECT, CHANGE IN OBJECT

The excitement of empirical research (especially the second time) evoked mixed feelings in the scholar, a sense of inadequacy for taking on such a task and for following in the footsteps of other scholars, the "greats" who had dealt with the same or similar themes. As has been admirably stated, "Every prolonged experience of detailed research leaves a kind of emotional scar on the researcher. Hands-on research is exhausting, but exciting. The first study on Middletown had lasted a year and a half, the authors' feelings alternating from enthusiasm to bored antipathy as the work progressed along its fatiguing way—through drafts, revisions, checks, rechecks, and finally, publication."[4] Now, however, the relationship between Robert Lynd and Middletown had changed, especially in his self-appointed role as its critical observer. In addition to the familiar conflict between the rational project of the scholar and the irrationality of the everyday life under investigation, the inhabitants of the city became lethargic, and reluctant to admit their own shortcomings.

The problems raised by the contrast between the objectives of the research and the reality of Middletown formed part of the typical antagonism of the relationship between observer and observed, reflecting the conflicts in Robert Lynd's own intellectual life: he had been born in the state of Indiana, but had severed his ties with it during the course of his intellectual formation. Lynd's return to Middletown, with all its problematic implications, dramatized once again the motivations of the scholar himself.[5]

At the time of the second research, Robert was thus a very different man than before. Just as Lynd's experience had changed him, Middletown, too, had been changed by the various important events in America during those years. President Roosevelt had given a new impulse to industrial development, with planning policies on the one hand, and incentives to production—and therefore to competition among businesses—on the other.[6]

Lynd returned to Middletown during the aftershocks of the Depression, that catastrophe that had devastated America and taught something valuable, it was hoped, to the American people. From all this, it came about that "the new research was thus more clearly than before focused on alterations in institutions and values as well as the conflicts generated by them and accompanying them."[7]

Lynd has been defined as an "American Marx" because he was interested in conflict, crisis, and transformation, and the resulting mutations in society.[8] Lynd's Middletown studies assessed America during the twentieth century just as Karl Marx had evaluated England during the nineteenth century. Sociology became a pretext for revealing the materialism of the time: the fetish of goods, the exalted nature of money, and the substitution of machines for workers. Moreover, the reality of American life during those years lent itself to the use, more or less implicit, of Marxian metaphors, even though the confines of Marxian categories were perhaps somewhat narrow even for Robert Lynd. *Middletown in Transition* highlights a series of concepts that gain weight in relation to their comparison with Marxian analysis of work capital and the classes. How determinant

Lynd's reading of Marx was in furnishing him new keys to unlocking the mysteries of the dynamics of capitalistic power and, in particular, of the "discovery" of the existence of the "X family," is even today the subject of scholarly debate. It is likely that Lynd found himself carried along by an internal process by which he would come to assume ever more radical positions. In part, this was owing to his progressive estrangement from the growing emphasis on empiricism in sociology at that time. It was not by chance, then, that his major theoretical work, *Knowledge for What?*, was published only one year after *Middletown in Transition.*[9]

THE STRUCTURE OF THE SECOND TEXT

The two young authors—for the text was signed by both, though the sole author this time was Robert—prudently decided to maintain the same structure in the second research as in the first.[10] Lynd came to the work with a deeper intellectual perception of facts and ideas. Both Robert and Helen were stirred by the experience and were sensitive to the "internal" arrangement of the volume as well as to its external presentation.

Though the six original areas—getting a living, making a home, training the young, leisure, religion, and community activities—were unchanged, the narrative structure was different. The content of the second volume was supported by a stronger conceptual framework providing scientific validation; but the formal changes were evident in two chapters that interrupted the continuity: the third chapter, "The X Family," and the twelfth, "The Spirit of Middletown," the two chapters that made it worthwhile for the Lynds' to visit Middletown once again in order to observe changes "from life" and to interpret them even at the risk of forcing a predetermined conclusion.

Aside from the two completely new chapters that will be discussed separately later, as they deserve, the innovations were minor and the six categories of daily and institutional activity remained the same, though in some cases they were expanded or reduced according to the quantity of material collected. Some significant examples: in the first volume, four chapters are dedicated to religion; in the second, only one, and the amount of space allotted to free time is reduced by half. In addition, *Middletown in Transition* gives greater space—three times that of the earlier volume—to two topics in particular, the governing machine and aid to the indigent.

The narrative structure of the second work is simpler than that of the first, which meant to include all of the citizens' activities, without exception. In the second study, the authors chose what and what not to include, and therefore its final written product, on the whole, turns out to be livelier and more powerfully clear and concise.

In this study two fundamental themes served as a basis for interpretation. The first concerned not only Middletown, but all sociological studies of the twenties and thirties that brought to light the growing standardization of life caused by the increasingly active role in local affairs played by national agencies of information diffusion and control—the mass media and the automobile, for example.[11] This persistent trend toward homogeneity came to influence the personal lives of individuals, bringing about new styles of life and fashion. The Lynds emphasized many times in both works the importance of the impact of mass society on the life of the individual.

The second theme, linked to the greater maturity of the theoretical ideas of the authors, concerned the formerly disregarded changes occurring in the workplace: unemployment, the training of a reserve industrial workforce composed of "internal" immigrants and African-Americans, and the changes happening in workers' consciousnesses. The Lynds had found an element of topical value: the discovery of the ways the population adapted to the crisis, paradoxically maintaining intact the desire for mobility in spite of the widespread reality of unemployment.

On the basis of these preliminaries, we can say that the questions the authors pose at the beginning of the work are, for the most part, answered. Perhaps it would be useful here to quote their precise formulation of these questions:

How much has the city actually changed through the experiences of boom and depression? Has the basic texture of this culture been tough enough to resist change and to remain intact? Have the different rates of change in different areas of living pointed out in the earlier study been maintained during this critical period? How has the deep faith of this people in the value of standing unaided on one's own feet withstood the experience of unprecedented public relief? Is their confident outlook on the future altered? Are people returning sharply to the old faiths, or are they moving out to embrace new ways of thought? What changes are being wrought in the young as compared with their elders, and in the various groups in the community? Has the depression created more sense of community, or new cleavages? Have the latent conflicts observed in 1925 within this culture pattern been sharpened or modified?[12]

During the first research, the couple stayed in Muncie for a good year and a half; in the second, Robert Lynd returned without his wife, and with five assistants stayed only one summer.[13] No new investigation was carried out and the sources noted earlier were used: statistical data, newspapers, as well as "participatory observation." Also, Lynd had at his disposal a large network of local spokespersons, some of them true "sources" (Bahr 1978).

While in the first study, the aim of two young authors, although critical, could be read between the lines—especially in the choice of background material that allowed the data to speak for themselves—in the second analysis their controversial position was evident and explicit.[14] Some critics of the book feel that it was assembled too quickly and that it had received much less conceptual, stylistic, and organizational attention (Fox 1983). Others feel that a certain methodological spontaneity counterpointed its greater interpretive breadth. The authors preselected the material they wanted to investigate and then communicated the results to the reader. It was not a systematic description (as in *Middletown*), but research into meanings and political intentions (Madge 1962). The study was less empirical but more interpretive, given the fundamental contribution of Marxist theory to the Lynds' conceptual framework.

For Stein, the two dimensions, methodological and interpretive, are well coordinated in *Middletown in Transition*: the Lynds achieved the difficult task of joining macrosociological theories to microsociological ones. The second research instructs the reader in a significant event of the thirties, the Depression, and in how this crisis upset the pattern of changes taking place. Viewed thus, interpretation of the data is focused and its sociological value noteworthy, though it should not be generalized, given that it refers to a local reality.[15]

Changes in Context

The quality of change, both general and specific, in the life of Middletown "ten years later," is not referred to in any of the scenarios provided at the beginning of *Middletown in Transition*. Changes were not extreme; rather, earlier tendencies already in progress were accentuated in such a way that a cumulative "Middletown spirit" could be discerned. Thus identified, the atmosphere of the city seemed, and perhaps was, stifling.

The loss of community spirit paralleled the city's growing concentration on business and consumption, and the work ethic was compromised as a means of individual promotion and social ascent. At the same time, relationships between people became ever more formal and calculated, with an increase in isolation, as had already been noticed by the Lynds in their first study. In crisis situations, people often attempt to defend themselves (not only in Middletown) by walling themselves up inside old certainties rather than learning new ways of adapting. Hence the Lynds' reference to Thomas's "four desires."[16]

To difficulties such as the scarcity of work and the increase in unemployment, the citizens of Middletown responded, therefore, by taking easy refuge in two typical responses of advanced capitalistic society: on one hand resorting to more liberal social habits, on the other tending more toward conventional practices, above all in the area of morality and religion. However, in the spirit of Lynd, one can ask if the latter response was a sign of a "reawakening" of conscience, or, on the contrary, was a mere tactic for circumventing the real issues.[17]

Certain aspects of life in Middletown remained unexplained by the two young authors in their first work; namely, the monopoly of the X family and the formation of a fringe population (African-American) in the city. Though the X family's monopoly appeared to force homogenization of the urban community, the inflow of ethnic minorities was clearly a sign of disintegration of an originally white, Anglo-Saxon, Protestant context. Both phenomena increased the city's fundamental disorientation.

Despite the crisis, the process of modernization had continued because of the public money that the New Deal had poured into the city. However, no new values had taken the place of the old ones. While the urban landscape had improved, the inhabitants had enclosed themselves in residential areas in which they found themselves trapped, isolated inside their own homes (this is the case even today in the residential areas near the college). As America emerged little by little from the Depression, the ideals of progress took hold: in this sense, however, the basic culture of Middletown remained the same. As already noted, there was no substitution of values, but rather, if anything, a buildup of conflicting values. The new coincided with the circumstantial: long-term policies were substituted with short-term responses in the name of social and individual survival.

In their disparagement of American society as found in Middletown, the authors are barely able to hide their regret that Muncie seemed not to have learned anything from their experience of the Depression. Ominously, the leadership of the community had not changed, but had come to be concentrated in the hands of a few—actually, a very few.[18]

The class contrasts, the rise of the ghetto, unemployment, hard work for women, and the easy escape into amusement and bars as described in *Middletown in Transition* was documented photographically in *Life* magazine. Margaret Bourke-White, a famous contemporary photographer, represented in her photographic survey (in her first job for *Life*) the different, contrasting social types in Middletown at the height of its difficulties. The population of Middletown was not and is not pleased with her interpretation. She portrayed quite accurately the extremes of the social hierarchy, from the ridiculous behavior of the newly rich who imported into Indiana such English-aristocratic modes of leisure as fox hunting (the "conspicuous consumption" of Veblen comes to mind), to the lives of poor whites from the mountains of Kentucky and Tennessee.[19]

The Lynds' second work on Middletown had completed a cycle in which the contradictions of the "American Empire" in the crucial years of its history were taking shape and growing uncontrollably.

NEW SOCIAL STRATIFICATION?

The themes of class—class struggle, painful subdivisions, internal rendings in the working class, the betrayal of the promise of socioeconomic "ascent"—clearly were focal points in the Middletown studies. In *Middletown in Transition*, the subject of social class is confronted directly only at the end of the volume—after a discussion of the X family's impact on the economic, social, and political reality of the city—in the famous chapter (that will be discussed separately) on the "spirit" of Middletown, the part of the book in which the story of big money, local power, and group interests unfolds.

The new orientation toward power seems fundamental, greatly important both for the interpretive-conceptual profile of Middletown, and for the social image of the city in that new phase of research. Inspired directly by Lewis Corey's book *The Crisis of the Middle Class*, Lynd saw the American middle class as a kind of "split personality," and applied this interpretation to the social situation in Middletown. Though Lynd attempted to take into account Middletown's individual traditions, he believed that the divisions there were caused by the increase in capital that put the "old" middle class of small businessmen and shop owners in opposition to a "new" middle class of people who were given jobs by the people in business. The two classes described as direct antagonists in the first volume become six classes in the second. Attempts to explain the disparity were not immune to oversimplification and even ambiguity.[20] Once again, the author's personal frustration communicates to us with indispensable immediacy the image of the social division we find in *Middletown in Transition*.

This is how the Lynds describe the collective dynamic of the city in transformation:

1. A very small top group of the "old" middle class is becoming an upper class, consisting of wealthy local manufacturers, bankers, the local head managers of one or two of the national corporations with units in Middletown, and a few well-to-do dependents of all the above, including one or two outstanding lawyers. (This class is largely identical with the group referred to throughout as the business control group and also with the group setting new and expensive standards in use of leisure.)

2. Below this first group is to be found a larger but still relatively small group, consisting of established smaller manufacturers, merchants, and professional folk (Middletown's outstanding "old" middle-class members in Corey's sense). . . .

3. Below Groups 1 and 2 come those who have been identified above as Middletown's own middle class in purely locally relative terms: the minor employed professionals, the very small retailers and entrepreneurs, clerks, clerical workers, small salesmen, civil servants—the people who will never quite manage to be social peers of Group 2 and who lack the constant easy contacts with Group 1 which characterizes Group 2.

4. Close to Group 3 might be discerned an aristocracy of local labor: trusted foremen, building trades craftsmen of long standing, and the pick of the city's experienced highly skilled machinists of the sort who send their children to the local college as a matter of course.

5. On a fifth level would stand the numerically overwhelmingly dominant group of the working class; these are the semiskilled or unskilled workers, including machine operatives, truckmen, laborers, the mass of wage earners.

6. Below Group 5 one should indicate the ragged bottom margin, comprising some "poor whites" from the Kentucky, Tennessee, and West Virginia mountains, and in general the type of white worker who lives in the ramshackle, unpainted cottages on the outlying unpaved streets. These are the unskilled workers who cannot even boast of that last prop to the job status of the unskilled: regular employment when a given plant is operating.[21]

The reader of the first volume on Middletown will realize that the inclusion of the sixth group in the classification above was marginal; it had its own dynamics that interacted only partially with the other components of Middletown. (It should be noted that the hillbillies, the people from the mountains of Kentucky and Tennessee, represented an ethnic group with separate cultural traditions from those of the original white, Anglo-Saxon, Protestant typical Middletown "stock." Moreover, the "poor whites" of the South, then as now, did not substantially alter the overall character of the city.) The only "new" class, relative to the earlier classification, was that of domestic help, which had appeared on the social scene not just in Middletown but everywhere in industrial society.

The white-collar workers formed (even for C. Wright Mills) part of the indistinct vast group that was partially and occasionally identified with the upper classes, sharing with them their patterns of consumption. In the Lynds' view, the growth of mass society and, more specifically, the increase of "tertiarization" (a social, political process linked to the development of the services sector) boded ill for an improved society in which indiscriminate conflict left little space for "democratic planning."

THE REEMERGENCE OF CLASS DIVISION

Beyond the apparent multiplication of social levels, one can discern in the Lynds' second book a different focus and a more fully articulated social map. A closer look suggests that the social divisions were based on a fundamental antagonism that was difficult to eradicate or transform. One example was the sort of relationship to capital that the three groups belonging to the middle and upper classes developed. As has already been noted in this regard (Cavalli 1970a), the factor of control assumed a fundamental importance: those groups that were not "subordinate" were agents of manipulation. The Lynds attempted to maintain their presentation of the divisions as set forth in the first volume while recognizing that the social structure during the thirties was becoming increasingly complex. Their final conclusions, viewed in the light of their (somewhat unorthodox) Marxian formulation, are really quite interesting.

The Lynds are noted for carrying out their interpretative effort at a time when social analysis was presented either in strictly economic terms or in the logic of a "neutral" social stratification in which the requisites of wealth, power, and prestige were mixed and distributed. The ideas at the heart of the Marxian formulation—class difference and conflict—are described in *Middletown in Transition* in reference to the means of production, while other aspects are less strictly formulated in such terms.

The Lynds' commentators did not agree with their classification for many reasons. Some emphasized its theoretical-methodological fragility; others evaluated it as conforming too much to Marxist interpretations that prevented recognition of certain aspects of social mobility in American society; still others praised the Lynds' capacity to combine and apply Marxian and anthropological categories to community studies.[22] In interpretive terms, the problem of the classes represented an essential point in the debate, together with the other connotative themes of the Lynds (especially Robert), consumption, power, and ideology—including the role of sociology in the construction of a new society.

In the second study, the authors noted the distinction between the upper echelon of the business class and the rest of its members, but chose not to emphasize that both groups acted together as a unit. In fact, in the development of their concept of class, the Lynds went beyond the Marxian criterion of salaried work as a fundamental element of differentiation between the two groups.[23] It was apparent that the worker-employees at all levels were subordinated to the "higher" level of the business class; but the Lynds went beyond this simple assumption. By analyzing the type of relationship that the various groups established with the agents of production—as coproducers or as managers—they explained how the process of control extended well beyond the workplace to insinuate itself into other institutional areas such as schools and churches.

Although the emphasis in *Middletown in Transition* (as in the earlier study) on "getting a living" was such that the workplace remained the most important institution in the city, the means of domination—applied toward ensuring control of work for capitalistic considerations—included many other terrains and social spheres. The manipulators in the conflict were in control of the means of production and the Lynds placed them in the business class, not in the middle class. This continuous vacillation between middle and upper class cannot be attributed exclusively to the authors' lack of theory and methodology, but to the objective reality of those years of rapid change.

The transformation of nineteenth-century capitalism from small competitive businesses to a small group of major capitalistic twentieth-century entrepreneurs is an important organizational principle of both volumes on Middletown. The major capitalists, who emerge in the second study as "an internal ruling group," dominate the small-business people through credit, and control workers through employment. According to Marx's predictions, capital would collide with crisis and emerge with even more power in America, and thus the Lynds' main objective became to identify the weak points of capitalism in that stage of its development in order to prepare such countermeasures as would guarantee a total social change.

Three important milestones had left an indelible mark on Middletown: in 1890, the principles of laissez-faire, small-business people competing with one another, defined the economic scene; during the twenties, there was a surge of monopolistic capitalism (the growth and the organization of contracted business); and finally, during the Depression in the thirties, state capitalism first emerged. The economic crisis had forced many small businessmen to declare bankruptcy while the more prominent businessmen solidified their control over the local economy. Conscious of their role as rulers of the destiny of Middletown, they put in place a program of economic development and social pacification that used the city government and its police force in order to exercise control over the population. For example, in order to induce General Motors to reopen their factories at Muncie in place of the one in Toledo, Ohio, which was on strike, the leaders of Middletown promised to release the automobile company from union obligations. Then they empowered the police, who were paid additional salaries, to keep the peace. The local union leaders accepted these humiliating conditions once they were guaranteed that new jobs would be given to unemployed union members.

During these years, the scholars of the Frankfurt School began to criticize advanced capitalist societies. It is not certain whether the Lynds were acquainted with the first texts by those authors at the time of the writing of *Middletown* I and II. It is probable, however, that such ideas were already in circulation in receptive intellectual climates like that of Columbia University.

Many of the Lynds' criticisms relative to the consumer system and mass society in Middletown recall the concept of the control by capital of all the forms of human life (Marcuse 1968b), and also more "molecular" modes of control (Foucault 1971). Especially in their second work, the Lynds traced the progress of the social and moral degradation in American society. Another stage in the loss of community is seen clearly by observing who controls the organization of movements and local associations. The decrease in the number of "controllers . . . operates to increase the sense of divisions within the group and of class lines as between the leaders and controllers and their immediate associates and, over against them, the large group of the manipulated and led."[24]

The result of this process of subdivision within groups and their loss of cohesion threatened to cut off a large section of the population from social life. From this point of view, "progressively as one comes down the social scale, the chance of becoming a lost individual, untied in any active sense to community-wide life and values, increases. One 'lives in' a town, one 'makes one's money there,' is part of its 'available labor supply,' rather than necessarily being an integral part of the town."[25]

The demise of community, the resulting solitude, and the loss of private, intimate values thus resurfaced. A recurring theme in the Frankfurters' view of power was that there was greater potential for control from above in a situation of potential social breakdown. The Lynds, once again, touched on a topic that was timely and important to the classic scholars of sociology. A comparison of what the couple produced in the twenties and thirties with what was written afterward on Middletown shows that their remarkable interpretive capacity overcame many of the defects in their work. Their penetration into the realities concerned prevailed over their lack of solid data. They offered a subtle, well-articulated and well-rounded treatment of the American life during those years that would shortly become the model of life for all of Western society.

The problem of the classes remained somewhat unclear, however. In both books, the classes remained fundamentally dichotomous, whereas, in fact, the Lynds may have had in mind merely an antagonism between blue-collar and white-collar workers. But even this distinction was effective only when intermediate elements were introduced. In substance, the authors remained entrenched in the dilemma: was class membership a result of destiny or of chance?

The first research on Middletown asserted that a person's destiny is determined by his or her birth into the working class or the business class. Afterward, however, the Lynds admitted to the factor of chance, especially in vocation: the young choose a lifetime vocation according to the information that they received from their parents, relatives, and friends. What, then, was the deciding factor, destiny or mere fortuitous circumstance?

In *Middletown in Transition*, the social situation seemed more complicated. Ten years after the first research, the Lynds confirmed again how the much vaunted, unexamined American values of social ascent had been altered:

One has traditionally been supposed to "go up in the world," "get ahead," "improve oneself," "arrive." Even in the 1920's it was apparently becoming slightly

harder even to get a job on the factory floor from which the ladder of opportunity rises. And once on the floor, the old single ladder reaching from the dead-
level of the working floor to the factory owner's comfortable chair has been
changing.[26]

The social ladder had been divided in half and it was impossible for the
qualified worker to leap the distance that separated the first from the second half.[27] New groups crowded together there that did not necessarily
come from worker backgrounds. Hence, the Lynds' famous thesis of
blocked mobility, which was later on criticized by Caplow and which took
as a reference point the "mythical year of 1890."[28]

Criticism by social historians was targeted at this generalization. In recent years, especially on the occasion of the Middletown III project, the
breakdown of opportunity following the growth of industrialization and
the mechanization of work has been reappraised. While the Lynds based
their research on limited sources of information,[29] more recent researchers
have attempted to trace the careers of individual workers by referring to
census data of cities in order to reconstruct upward and downward mobility, and sociologists have conducted retrospective interviews. The results
of this research show a stable rate of ascending mobility from blue collar
to white collar, in terms of both the parent-child legacy and the individual, personal career. Thus it seems that social mobility has been relatively
constant in industrial America from 1850 to today.

In the sixties, one community study on Newburyport, Massachusetts,
conducted by a historian[30] of the "new school," even reached the surprising conclusion that there was more mobility in that town in the nineteenth century than today. Again the Lynds' thesis of blocked mobility was
disclaimed and this time with detailed comparisons. The couple's research
was thus shown to contain fundamental methodological inadequacies.

One reason for their misjudgment was the fact that the Lynds had not
studied the historical origins of the working force in Middletown: in
Muncie, as in Newburyport, the new workers were not mainly déclassé
artisans. The industrial working force was actually composed of men and
women who had little to lose in terms of original status: emigrants from
rural America or the Old World.

According to one group of social historians, the advent of consumerism took place during the twenties and even more during the thirties, while automobile purchases underlined the acceptance of middle-
class values and gave many workers the illusion of vertical mobility. This
was true especially for women: they were more often employed than during the previous ten years and their numbers had increased in the clerical
sectors while diminishing in the industrial sector. But, by and large, the
only professional fields open to capable women were teaching and medi-

cine. Another interesting fact is that the number of married women relative to 1920 had grown, and positions in the workplace had increased for
them as well. In the thirties, on the other hand, the relative position of
women in the working world appeared to decrease.

Competition for jobs for men was already evident at various levels: in
some sectors, such as teaching, married women were no longer employed; in
addition, there was the tendency—with the exception of piecework—to
assign new working positions first to unemployed men and the remainder to
women. In factory work, therefore, this competition was especially evident.

The average Middletowner believed that women were privileged to
remain within the walls of their homes. The crisis obstructed their timid
efforts at emancipation through work outside the home. Whether or not
women working outside the home was an indicator of change in the city's
habits would be reviewed later. And in any case, those women who
wanted to do something different than the types of work offered in
Middletown could only "migrate" elsewhere.

With their usual acuity, the authors identified the exclusion of women
(even women belonging to the business world) from the environments of
masculine work, where not just ability but also an aggressive, competitive
spirit was called for. This situation represented another aspect of the de-
generation of community: women (and mothers) who wanted to do
something different than what had been predetermined as "women's
work" were forced to leave the city. Their departure (and thus their rebellion against community codes of behavior), as well as the stigma attached
to such rebellion, was far from painless even for the men. Here is where
the individual personality came up against the limits of the context. The
discourse of the Lynds', at this point, transcends gender, even if we know
that the woman who did not conform was judged for being "different"
from the community she had left.[31]

PARTICULAR AREAS

As stated earlier, the principal activity in Middletown was (and still is)
"getting a living," which determined who one was, who one knew, and
what one could hope to aspire to. The various vital aspects of life were
shaped by what one did to earn a living and what that earning permitted
him or her to buy.

In the years last studied by the Lynds, the working class in Middletown
was recruited from first- or second-generation farming people. These self-
sufficient individuals were forced into the competition of the job market,
where the alienation of assembly-line work heightened their sense of loss
of identity in a world dominated by the ideology of increased standard of
living for all. Their wishes were also shaped by the prevalent belief that

the possession of an automobile would guarantee them a sort of equality in relation to others. The Lynds emphasized how private industry continually tempted working people, inviting them to find remedies to their unhappiness through increasing their possessions and consuming more material goods. The workers were not told, however, that the results of this choice would be isolation, insecurity, and frustration. The reality of working conditions nullified the vaunted idea that anyone can rise to any height in America.

As already seen ten years earlier, the working people in the industries of Middletown were increasingly composed of unskilled labor on one side, and on the other, of business men and technicians who would rise above the working class. The changes occurring in the workplace dictated in great part the deterioration of other aspects of life in Middletown.

The descriptions in the "Making a Home" chapter of *Middletown in Transition* are lively and timely, and are valid even in today's Muncie. Though marriage was often postponed because of the insecurity generated by the economic crisis, especially for the intermediate, less economically consolidated social groups, the dominant reality of Middletown private life was and remains matrimony. In the Lynds' words, "Middletown is a marrying city."

Not incidentally (it might even happen to a visitor to the city today):

The unmarried members of the research staff, coming from New York with its larger proportion of young bachelor men and women, felt the pressure of pairwise activity. One felt it all the way from such simple matters as the dearth of pleasant places to eat if one did not have a home, through the customary activities that constitute "spending the evening" in Middletown.[32]

And the text continues:

Middletown has developed, as it has grown in the last generation and particularly since the World War, small bachelor apartments, more commercial eating places, and other facilities for living in "single blessedness." But in a city of this size, remote from a metropolitan center, the alternatives are still apparently sufficiently limited to make marriage decidedly "the thing to do," and to do young.[33]

With the crisis, the divorce rate fell because it became economically impossible for a husband to maintain an ex-wife with alimony payments. The birthrate decreased too; having babies was postponed for a more favorable time. The segregation of the sexes continued; there were actually two separate cultures, one for men and one for women. High-school girls did not want to do housework, which always weighs heavily on women, but wanted to work and have their independence. Private attitudes during the Depression, however, did not necessarily last; everything was temporary. For example: "Such momentary access of stature in the family as women may have achieved during the depression may be wiped out by the slow relative loss of opportunity which women appear to be suffering in the male-dominated world of business, professions, and industry."[34]

However much the education of the young ("training the young") was important in Middletown, as it is everywhere in America, as a means of social ascent for its youngest members, the social changes that were underway were still not stabilized. Despite the pressures on young people in Middletown, two types of positive change can be noted: the first was the growing importance of the city's "X College" during the previous ten years. Moreover: "Had Middletown been a 'college town' in any observable sense in the fall of 1923 when the city was selected for study, the study would not have been made there."[35]

In the following decade, under the influence of the X family, the original teachers college was transformed into a college that recruited students aggressively. In June 1936, it issued 22 master of arts degrees and 171 bachelors degrees, in addition to 141 teaching-qualification certificates awarded after a two-year course. An elegant building, costing $2,500,000 and competing in attractiveness with the best college campuses and universities in the state, had been constructed on the land of the old property purchased for $35,000 in 1918. The elegant residential quarter of the city was moved from the East End toward the west, into that area that an ambitious group of building speculators in this city of extremely flat prairies hopefully called "university hill." The Lynds noted the widespread pride and enthusiasm that Middletown citizens felt about their college, which is today's Ball State University.

Another element of change in the training of the young linked two contrasting values: individualism and conformity. Education based on individual differences, the Lynds wrote, "introduces sharp conflicts at this time when the local culture is putting renewed stress on elements that make for solidarity and unanimity."[36] The Lynds argued that this individual-centered concept of education no longer responded to the new necessities of adapting the young to a society that had to be as unified as possible. This was true, both in times of recession and during economically prosperous periods, because social and cultural complexity was increasing. Finally, Middletown also faced the phenomenon of mass education and the consequent necessity of using increasingly standardized methods.[37] The Middletown teachers were at the center of these disagreements, and there was a continual jockeying for position among many of them.

There had been few changes in the use of free time, though the authors noticed that there was an increase in free time organized by associations with funds provided by the federal government. The Lynds put forth a question about this: how long would this trend continue before the return of self-directed use of free time?

The legalization of the consumption of alcoholic beverages was another significant influence on how people used their leisure time, although the importance of drinking, alone or with others,[38] was more a part of working-class than of business-class behavior.

The authors did not seem to be favorably impressed that the reading rate of the Middletown population had doubled. They preferred to see defects in the "imprudent choice of texts" and wondered whether people would read as much after the Depression, when more costly entertainment would be possible.

In a culture in which people felt frustrated and unrealized without a high standard of living, they wanted jobs that promised more money for buying easy leisure.

In their reexamination of religious practice, the Lynds emphasized that religion paralleled consumption as a source of compensation for the insecurity of facing a complex world. Consequently, the roles and forms of Christianity in Middletown were based on three points: making sure one was on the side of the "righteous," the divinity of Jesus Christ, and the promise of eternal life. The need for security was so great because many were not able to accept the rapid changes in their lives. Religion became an example of how people needed "vital lies" to keep themselves going in moments of crisis, and reaffirmed and reinforced their need for emotional stability.

The Lynds' view of religion as an illusion is another instance of Marx's influence on them. Conspicuous consumption and religion had a "consolatory" function, particularly for those who, like the inhabitants of Middletown, did not have many choices, or chances for happiness, unless they decided to leave. For the Lynds, therefore, religion was characterized by a strong resistance to change. The difference between this reality and the realities of family relations, education, and the use of free time was clearly visible: in those areas some change was perceptible, even if the interpretation of it was ambiguous. Religion also played a part in the city's attitudes toward civic activities and public affairs. Local politicians were constrained to pay lip service to popular religious opinion, a contradiction that often weighed heavily on their careers.

There had not been any particularly illuminating innovations in public administration in the previous ten years in Middletown, despite the emphasis placed by the administrators on new police patrols with radiotelephones, hourly parking, a street-cleaning machine, and other "novelties." As usual, the Lynds' portrayal is vivid and timely, especially for those who know Muncie well. In many respects, there is a feeling that the source of change has gone underground, that things are changed but that a fundamental mystery remains, independent of all the events that have characterized the history of that portion of America.

Nonetheless, the Lynds tended to minimize the aspects of nonconformity in Middletown: for example, they could have explored the increase in beer drinking and gambling with the onset of the Depression. The data gathered by the Lynds indicated that there never was a wave of local criminality provoked by the Depression. If this was true, it was also true that there was a certain amount of criminal activity, though on a small scale, that took as its model the vice and public corruption belonging to the underworld crime of big cities like Chicago during the twenties and thirties. One should not forget either that Indiana was John Dillinger country. His bank-robber band never actually threatened Muncie directly, but his influence was certainly felt in a dramatic way. Finally—and here it would be interesting to dedicate more space to the situation—the case of Mayor George R. Dale demonstrated how it was practically impossible for a "clean" politician to govern Middletown. This man had been applauded at a national level for his struggle against the Ku Klux Klan and had the virtue of being an honest, courageous man, but at the same time, the defect of not being a "professional politician" and of not understanding the art of compromise. It was relatively easy for his enemies to get rid of him as mayor by first accusing him of being involved in the illegal whiskey trade (the accusations were proved later to be false) and then by continuing to invent charges against him so that he was not reelected in 1934.

In the pages in *Middletown in Transition* about the public administration, we note the authors' bitterness about the general political scene in the city and in all of America. Their criticism ranges from the particular to the general and finally becomes bitterly polemical against the entire political system: "Middletown jogs along in its civic affairs, riding uneasily with one foot on the back of each of the ill-fated horses of democratic symbol and urgent reality."[39] The attitudes of the people of Middletown toward politics were divided: party ties were expressed at a national level, but were weak or nonexistent in local affairs. As a result of New Deal policies, businessmen were beginning to feel that the federal government was no longer with them, but rather, had turned against them. The conviction was thus formed in the city that it must act as a separate entity in order to preserve its competitive advantage over other centers of production.

The X Family

At the beginning of the famous chapter on the X family, the Lynds explain (though not very clearly) why they have not taken into consideration the power of the family in the first volume: "Since *Middletown* was published, some local people have criticized it for underplaying the role of the

X family in the city's life." And they also quote a local source, always prudently citing the original reference: "It doesn't seem to me that the importance of the X family in the city has been adequately portrayed. One must be careful, though, in this criticism, as a considerable portion of the philanthropy bestowed by them on [Middletown] has been done since the 1925 study."[40] In addition, the authors explain, the richest families in the first study were not considered as a separate group because they were an integral part of the business class. They continue defensively:

Whether or not the earlier study was entirely right in so largely grouping them with the rest of the business class, certainly no local prompting was necessary in 1935 to call attention to their overshadowing position. For, after ten years' absence from the city, one thing struck the returning observer again and again: the increasingly large public benefactions and the increasing pervasiveness of the power of this wealthy family of manufacturers, whose local position since 1925 is becoming hereditary with the emergence of a second generation of sons.[41]

They deny that the X family's influence had to be "unmasked," since it was quite easily perceptible to the eye of any attentive observer (such as they were). We shall return later to the "unspoken" aspects of their intuition.

The subtitle of the chapter dedicated to the X family, "A Pattern of Business-Class Control," unequivocally indicated the authors' intention of using the family as an example in their description (and denunciation) of the mechanisms of "total" power in the city. Apart from the fundamental antagonism that divided the city in two, and even considering all the nuances within the new social stratifications, it was very likely that there was a "power elite" within the business class itself. The X family stood at the summit of the pyramid of this elite. In the ten years between *Middletown* and *Middletown in Transition*, this wealthy family, which had already been well established, had increased its financial power as well as its control over citizens' activities.

In less than thirty pages the authors summarize the problem, in what can be considered a book within a book, or rather, a treatise on power as a paradigm of the American situation. In choosing not to furnish much information on the history of the family, it is almost as if the authors wish to intimate that the family's power is hidden, even though their name is known, and that they behave according to norms that transcend the structure, the kind of action, and even the uniqueness of the social position at stake.

Since the Lynds' book does not provide much in terms of a history of the family, readers might be interested in learning something about the genealogical line of the family relative to the history of the blossoming of American capitalism.

The five Ball brothers (Edmund Burke Ball, Frank Clayton Ball, George Alexander Ball, Dr. Lucius L. Ball, and William Charles Ball) moved to Muncie from Buffalo, New York, in 1887. It was the time of rapid expansion in the natural-gas business, which the brothers wanted to take full advantage of in order to establish their glass-works factories in Muncie. By the turn of the century, the Ball plant in Middletown was considered the biggest producer in the world of jars for preserves. These astute businessmen invested in other important commercial ventures in the city, such as a factory for automobile transmission parts, a meatpacking plant, a bank, the airport, the biggest department store in the city, and a daily newspaper, the *Morning Star*. During the Depression, George Alexander Ball obtained control of a financial empire that included ownership of the railroads passing through Middletown. The local teachers college and the community hospital were named after the Balls because of their contributions to those institutions. Most of the philanthropic organizations in the city were financed and perhaps also dominated by the "benevolent" family.

When Robert Lynd returned to Middletown in 1935, two of the original founders of the dynasty of the marmalade jars, Frank Clayton Ball and George Alexander Ball, were still alive. The members of the second generation, E. Arthur Ball, Edmund F. Ball, William Hudson Ball, and, before his early death in 1936, Frank Eliot Ball, were assuming roles of command in the family's businesses.[42]

The Lynds' description in the first pages of the text revealed neither resentment nor criticism, even though they had already stated their intention to censure the family's use of power in Middletown. In a few words, they describe the family's fortunes as linked to the "mythical" adventures of the pioneers, whose virtues the Balls appeared to incarnate: courage, individualism, and rectitude. They had achieved the American dream of great success from humble beginnings.

The boys had been born on a farm in Ohio, whence the family had migrated during the Civil War by wagon to another farm in western New York State. After receiving a common-school education, the five boys scattered to make their way in the world—one as a farm hand and timber cutter, one to become a doctor, others to develop a small business manufacturing fishing kits. When the latter plant was destroyed by fire, the brothers turned to the glass business.[43]

Nonetheless, the Lynds were chiefly interested in showing how the power of the family had grown in the city, until, in the Lynds' opinion, they had achieved control over all activities and the lives of the individual citizens as well. Others had already noticed the X family's importance in the life of the city, but this is part of a controversy that clashes not only with this particular case, but with every scientific "discovery" and intuition in research.

The Lynds characterized the X family as autocratic and arbitrary. In their opinion, "Middletown has, therefore, at present what amounts to a reigning royal family."[44] In their domination over all areas identified by the Lynds—in particular, getting a living, finance, legal activities, industry, and commerce—the Balls followed all the conventional rules of the game with just enough margin of probity to satisfy the ethics of their Protestant heritage. They were certain they were acting in the best interests of everyone according to the traditional economic theory that asserts that if factories do not give profits to their owners, then they are not productive and the community itself will suffer.

In addition, the Balls encouraged development in the city by contributing to, among other things, the growth of the college. Young people would therefore be taught by educators and teachers who were agreeable to the family. There was no true suppression to speak of, but it was understood that the educational institution would be submitted to continuous scrutiny by the family. They made donations to the YMCA that offered activities for children and families, and encouraged certain congenial religious practices, especially those that tended to make the citizens responsible and "devoted" to the Ball family.

But what did the people in Middletown think of the X family? For the Lynds, the criterion of class division was more valid here than anywhere else: the working-class reaction to the power of the X family was opposite to that of the business class: the former resented the power of the X family while the latter admired it. The Lynds made it clear that the attitude of the workers was not dictated by personal motives, but by the structural inequality that separated them from the world that decided their fates. One incisive comment of a Middletown citizen is recorded: "Working-class people here pretty generally dislike the X's. They feel they pay scant wages and then give things to Middletown. I ought to know, for I live down among them and I work for the X's."[45] For various reasons, the business class held the opposite opinion. It "either embraces or huddles toward the X's because they know that the system through which they earn their salaries, receive dividends, buy new Buicks, and send their children to college depends upon the enterprise of men like these."[46] The women who were part of the business class tended to have a more personal, emotional attitude toward the X family than did the men.

Success was traditionally central to the ideas of the white, Anglo-Saxon, Protestant population of Middletown. The attitudes of the business class changed from the first to the second generation of "patrons of the city." A family's or a person's prominence was different when their wealth was derived from personal initiative as opposed to inheritance or to a class system of privilege.

Nevertheless, the authors perceived that the family's power base might shift through the accidental death of the X family's young heir apparent. The family's influence would then be much less direct because of the possible transfer of their business interests from their community to activities outside the city. The Lynds' prophecy was destined to prove true: the Balls' presence is hardly noticeable now, although the marks left by their activities are indelible.

The Sky over Middletown

As many know, Gustave Flaubert had meant to write a dictionary of commonplaces: he had thus annotated, classified, and analyzed the totality of values accepted by the bourgeoisie of his time. In the last analysis, perhaps reference to the "spirit of Middletown" recalls the project of that illustrious literary giant that was, alas, never carried out. This work belonged to the same genre, though the comparison may remain somehow lopsided.

What did the average person in Middletown think? What were his or her real opinions on morality, religion, the family, business affairs, society, politics, the world? What, in short, was his or her conception of (ideal and lived) life, and how was its expression received by conventional opinion: with approval or condemnation?

Robert and Helen dig down into this opaque mass in an effort to go beyond the intrinsic limitations of their research work.[47] In this part of the book, which covers almost one hundred pages, the Lynds approached the most elusive cultural symbols and replied to criticism of their own analysis.[48]

However, the twelfth chapter—unlike the third ("The X Family")— was strategically placed toward the end of the book, before the "prospects" and the appendixes. The description of the "spirit of Middletown," together with that of the power of the X family, made the second study even more famous among scholars than the first: this chapter is a mass of observations that were not particularly easy to organize. Conclusions sometimes seem forced and oversimplified, though as usual, the Lynds' writing talent is evident: no page is lacking in acute observation and stimulating intuition.

Basically, the chapter is a classic example of the practice of the technique of "participant observation." In their illustration of the "spirit" of the city, the Lynds were aware of the difficulties caused by generalizations and distortions, often resulting from "cultural" analysis, but at the same time, they do not seem to doubt the usefulness of their considerations; they accept the risks. The Lynds found that, for the people of Middletown, the familiar, the habitual, the taken-for-granted—all went toward providing standards for acceptance or refusal. In other words, the elements that were "extraordinary" in relation to accepted, daily routines were subjected to (in Middletown as elsewhere) a kind of collective dismissal. So much so that, "those persons who most nearly exemplify the local stereotypes thrive, are 'successful,' and 'belong'; while dropping away behind them are others who embody less adequately the values by which Middletown lives, down to the community misfits who live meagerly in the shadow of frustration and unpopularity."[49] This last type of personality, defined by the Lynds as "deviant," was likely to be particularly unpopular in a context where the "normal" and the "common" were esteemed, the deviant "bohemian" lifestyle categorically rejected in favor of a conventional "philistine" one.

Naturally, it was not easy for these researchers to penetrate very far past the bounds of lawful or permitted behavior. In this sense, the cultural universals used by the Lynds came to clash with a dynamic, historic vision of culture with a subtle range of individual variations, and had to include those simplifications necessary for the identification of a more variegated picture of reality.

VALUES ACCEPTED, VALUES REFUSED

In order to be accepted as a good citizen of Middletown, one needed certain basic qualities: for example, a good temperament, which, according to an old Anglo-Saxon notion, was more important than intelligence. In addition, one had to be "a good fellow" and "a good neighbor," uncomplicated and without airs, a "booster" who believed in the future of Middletown and contributed to it in a conscious way, as opposed to the "knocker," the critic who saw obstacles, hindrances, and discouragement everywhere. One should be like everybody else, never go it alone, or make choices that had not been proved correct. Faith in progress, in community spirit, in individual success—good omens for collective prosperity—were important for sustaining daily life. Moreover, for the people of Middletown, the American economy and politics were the best in the world, which until then had produced the best results. In addition, family values allowed the "natural" segregation of the sexes: women were "purer" than men; they lacked a practical spirit; culture was their domain, and production the men's.

American pragmatism was apparent in regard to religious values. The churches satisfied many social needs for companionship. In fact, a community without a church was not worthy to be considered such, and church attendance was a noble activity to be encouraged. Pastors were meant to deal with religious questions only and not to worry themselves with business or politics. Protestantism was better than Catholicism.

Negative values included the opposite of all the values stated above and thus every type of personality that was different from the norm: for example, the pessimist or the nonjoiner who refused to collaborate. Any innovation in art, literature, or ideas that did not contain some sensational, spectacular novelty was deprecated.

Social types who were disapproved of were "radical" or "exotic" (this latter is a word much used even today to indicate a European or someone from the South). Eventually, this mental list would come to include anyone who criticized American institutions, such as social planners, intellectuals, snobs, revolutionaries, Russians, pacifists, presumptuous people, non-Protestants, Jews, and African-Americans (these last three because they were different: "not quite our sort"). Whoever was perceived as a nonconformist incurred the odium of the community. Social types who were judged unfavorably were considered dangerous promoters of disorder: sooner or later, Middletown openly or tacitly eliminated them.

These notes have only attempted to outline the characteristics and convictions of the people of Middletown that the Lynds provided. Two main points were specified by the authors out of the mass of facts, opinions, and subjects. The first concerned the "cycle of life" typical for the individual men and women of Middletown. The second, more important and ambitious, was linked to the changes occurring in Middletown during and since the Depression, along with certain predictions for the future. The Lynds approached new structural themes such as class, politics, city government, information diffusion, and so on. For this reason, the chapter closed with a loss of focus, dispersing into many directions that were difficult to reshape into a coherent whole.

THE PROGRAM OF LIFE FOR MEN AND WOMEN

In one fell swoop, the Lynds touched on a topic of extreme interest and relevance. Unfortunately, this "biographical process," usually so fruitful in qualitative sociological analysis, was not particularly developed by the Lynds either here or elsewhere.

The Lynds outlined a life cycle, including the various stages of the journey and the stopping places along the way, that characterized the destiny of the Middletowner. From infancy to old age, he would attempt to stay on the side of the right, thereby legitimizing surrounding values. Life was viewed as a smooth course on which no accidents were allowed that might disrupt the journey. The Middletowner was a man with many good qualities, in sum, but without too many nonconformist characteristics that might run counter to that life's progression.

What do we find if we pass from the masculine viewpoint to that of women?

For a Middletown woman the measurable kind of success is somewhat less coercive and success lies in a different sphere. Her success as wife and mother is measured in terms of her husband and children. She may be quiet and unaggressive socially and interested primarily in her family; but she should have some interest in club work, church work, social life, and philanthropy, be responsive to other people and to good causes, and helpful and friendly. In her case, too, there are certain desirable negative emphases, toning her down to the "womanly" type and to a position secondary to that of men; a woman should not be too intelligent, too witty, too aggressive and independent, too critical, or too different. She should not want a career, and should not compete with men, but rather back them up. The woman who markedly infringes any of these taboos may have both men and her own sex arrayed against her.[50]

The outline of a woman's life stands out only by complementing a man's: an indication of the lack of female emancipation in Middletown and at the same time of the atmosphere of conservatism that joined and separated the two sexes. The Lynds should have explored this more thoroughly in connection with dominant and emerging values.

AFTER THE DEPRESSION: BETWEEN TOLERANCE AND INSECURITY

In the various spheres of life in the city during and after the Depression, tolerance seemed to increase somewhat in certain areas, such as religion, education, and the press, while in others—in particular, union activities and national political issues—there seemed to be less of it. It is not clear from the text what sort of "tolerance" the Lynds mean: superficial, defensive, or repressive? In the section of the "Middletown spirit" chapter immediately following the discussion about men and women, conformity and tolerance appear as very similar traits: tolerance seems to be mere passivity, passive acceptance, or prudence (resilience?) that might even be seen as a loss of fighting spirit, of world-weariness. Stiff-upper-lip endurance, "a greater insistence upon conformity," and insecurity were part of the crisis and its unmanageableness. Thus, the conflict already latent in the culture of Middletown was "rendered more acute, namely, that mentioned above in the discussion of the successful businessman between the power-dominance-aggression values of the business world and the affectional-lovable-human values of family and interpersonal life."[51]

In addition, Middletown was anything but tolerant toward foreign-policy issues and their possible ideological effects within America. The

Soviets, the communists, and the socialists all were seen as enemies to shoot down, a collective demon that corroded both system and conscience.

Nonetheless, the impasses of conformity, defensiveness, and insecurity as guiding values of social and individual action eventually came to be surmounted by that orientation toward the future that de Tocqueville and others had recognized as a great American virtue.

The ten years between 1925 and 1935 brought various changes, more of them in certain spheres than in others. On the whole, the number of contrasting values increased but their quality did not develop decisively in one direction or another. There had been a moment in the history of Middletown when its symbols and beliefs ran parallel with its dreams and the realities of everyday life. In the years of the economic boom, progress was apparent and touched everyone, though of course some profited from it more than others. With the Depression, on the other hand,

the distance between the symbolic universe of belief and the pragmatic universe of everyday action has widened. They have again floated abruptly apart, and so far apart as to demand of Middletown *either* that it apply its customary formula and blindly deny that the gap has actually widened, or at least regard it as merely a temporary interruption; *or* that it revise this high-floating world of symbols, re-stating it in humbler and less hopeful terms so as to re-locate it closer to everyday reality; *or* that it accept as normal the fact of living in an enhanced state of tension because of the unwonted permanent remoteness of the two planes.[52]

The symbolic ceiling above Middletown had collapsed: there was no longer hope for everyone, but only a reality shaped by the will and actions of the power elite. Dreams themselves were reduced to contingencies and wonder had been exchanged for consumer objects; or their range was restricted to the parameters of the possible, limited to the triviality of the objects within reach: in short, betrayed by themselves (Caillois 1990).

CHAPTER 4

Muncie and Middletown:
The Controversy About the Perrigo Case

The "Message in the Bottle"

Although the Lynds do not dedicate much space to the X (Ball) family, the reader senses that the chapter "The X Family," placed at the beginning of the book, has significance beyond the pages of *Middletown in Transition*. Actually, this chapter is the tip of an iceberg; there is much more going on in it than it seems. What do the pages we have reveal and what do they hide? Above all, the case of the X family is an excellent example of capitalistic power structure,[1] particularly of the joint power between monopoly and state in America in the 1930's. Robert never finished the book about power that he intended to write—although this chapter could be seen as constituting the beginning of such a book, and there are many scattered essays that might also have contributed to it, and that indicate, in any case, the direction of his thought.

Aside from this, another, much more disturbing truth for the contemporary researcher is that he or she finds in the Lynds' book not only treasures, but also detritus, black holes, points of no return. Today, with hindsight, it seems like a message in a bottle, which in no way diminishes the untarnished fame of the Lynds as intellectuals and ideologists seriously committed to field research.

Like a deep-sea diver, I had to decide whether to leave what I found where it lay or to bring it to the surface. I could toss the metaphorical bottle back to memory's muddy bottom; on the other hand, to do so might have been a pointless act of piety. I told myself that the Lynds did not need to hide anything in order to maintain their reputation intact; nor am I someone with that sort of mission. If anything, my duty goes in the opposite direction: in the spirit of scientific investigation, to become familiar with the material I found and, without holding anything back, to make it available for study by others.

Before the Lynds started their second campaign of research in the field, someone else in Muncie had begun to think about what had happened meanwhile in Middletown. This person was Lynn Perrigo, a teacher from Muncie who had left the city to study for a Ph.D. in history at the University of Colorado. In fact, the title of his dissertation is "Muncie and Middletown, 1924 to 1934." Although the tone of this short paper is moderate, the intention was polemical with regard to the Lynds. Perrigo divides his work into the same six areas chosen by the Lynds (getting a living, making a home, training the young, using free time, engaging in religious practices, engaging in community activities), and examines the changes in each of these spheres, trying to point out aspects that the Lynds had overlooked or failed to mention. I found this manuscript, which is a sort of miniature "counter-Middletown," in the historical archives of the Bracken Library in Muncie. It was a lucky discovery for my work.

All things considered, it seems important to discuss such unusual material and to summarize it fairly. I think, then, that the only way to proceed is to take up the various points as they are set forth in the Perrigo paper. As the title suggests, with its opposition between Muncie and Middletown, the paper follows two lines of inquiry: On one hand it examines the first volume of the Lynds' work, or better, the intellectual operation that underlies it—the analysis of a reality and the construction of the image of a midwestern city, as seen by two urbanized intellectuals. On the other hand, it concentrates on the changes that took place between 1924, the year in which the young couple began their research, and 1936.

Perrigo did not know then that the Lynds were about to continue their research, or rather nothing in his paper shows that he knew this. In retrospect we can say that if they had not written their second book, *Middletown in Transition*, there would probably have been a lot less interest in the Perrigo manuscript, which would have been lost among the vast literature on Middletown available only to the specialist (as in fact this manuscript is) by special permission. Some American social scientist interested in the question of Muncie/Middletown would perhaps have mentioned the "new elements" it introduced—the importance of the X family, or of the college, how the locals reacted to the Lynds' book, new data for the spheres of activity during the Great Depression, and so on.

But it is useless to reconstruct a scenario that never happened. The Lynds did repeat their research on Middletown, and it was very well received in sociological circles, if not by the public. In fact, it was probably a greater success than the first volume. On the other hand, it is also legitimate to ask some questions about the relationship between Perrigo and the Lynds and the impact that Perrigo's modest but pointed work may have had on the Lynds' complex sociological study. How central is the role of the local informer and why don't the Lynds ever mention him by name? Is it done out of respect for a request by Perrigo for anonymity, or is it a deliberate attempt to hide a source that was essential to their work, however slight its real contribution? Here are two passages in which Perrigo's name is conspicuously absent: "Since *Middletown* was published, some local people have criticized it for underplaying the role of the X family in the city's life." A comment in this vein by a local source, quoted in a note at the bottom of the same page as the above statement, went like this: "It doesn't seem to me that the importance of the X family in the city has been adequately portrayed. One must be careful, though, in this criticism, as a considerable portion of the philanthropy bestowed by them on [Middletown] has been done since the 1925 study."[2] These are Lynn Perrigo's words.

Paradoxically, the controversy between Perrigo and the Lynds erupted only long after Robert Lynd's death. As we shall see, the question was probably never cleared up, but at least Robert was spared further disappointment in connection with this issue. He had believed in the democratic ideals of his America, and he had been so deeply disillusioned that he chose silence and early retirement. In any case, this type of posthumous controversy tends to run its course once the real protagonists have disappeared: Robert S. Lynd and Lynn Perrigo can no longer have their say.

The "thorny" context in which the debate developed is interesting. When a group of sociologists headed by Theodore Caplow (who had been one of Lynd's students at Columbia) decided to replicate the field research with the project Middletown III, the members of the group fanned out in many directions in the search for new sources and ideas. Indeed, it was an ambitious and courageous undertaking to comb over a field that had already been thoroughly researched twice, many years before, and that had given posterity two classic sociological studies on America before the Second World War. Caplow's group placed no limits on the criticism that might be leveled at the Lynds, from every point of view.

Indeed, in the new context—where new concepts and theories with respect to the Lynds came into play—the chance to criticize the discussion of "power" in *Middletown in Transition* from an insider's viewpoint seemed like a unique opportunity. In particular, a rereading of the supposedly exclusive control over the city exercised by one family, documented by other sources, offered the sociologists the immediate opportunity to contrast their findings with those of the Lynds and to distance themselves from the original research. This was a chance to revise the original construct with the help of interpretations and categories very different from those originally used. In this way, the critical potential of the earlier investigation was diminished by the discovery of another source that had already discussed the same subject, and had perhaps even anticipated its thesis. Even the sociological importance of the Lynds' affirmations acquired another tone; their investigation took on a different validity. Certainly, as we shall see in the reconstruction of the controversy that follows, the events also lend themselves to interpretations that diminish the reputation of Lynd as a research sociologist without fault or fear. If we read the evidence as we would journalistic information, the doubts remain.

BETWEEN REALITY AND IMAGE

Lynn Perrigo's manuscript consists of an introduction, a brief analysis of the six categories already considered by the Lynds, and the latter's development in the reality of Muncie. Once again, the categories proposed (with critical discussion and "further developments" for each) are getting a living, making a home, training the young, engaging in religious practices, engaging in community activities. The paper discusses two new themes: "ecology of the city" and "the Ball brothers' demesne." Finally, there is a brief conclusion in which the author's ambivalence toward Lynd's work (for he refers to *Middletown* only in reference to Robert, not Helen) is evident: its "discoveries" and forced interpretations, its cynicism and, at the same time, its lucidity.

Although I do not want to make too many suggestions before I discuss Perrigo's own position, I do want to say that his work is not, strictly speaking, a sociological study; his theoretical base is too limited. In fact, after the exquisite narrative of the Lynds, we are struck by Perrigo's simplistic treatment and his adaptation of the Lynds' categories of interpretation. But there is something more. If we overlook the limited scientific value of the work, which the author himself recognized, some of Perrigo's notations are interesting because they undoubtedly influenced Lynd's second study of Middletown, defined the spirit in which it was carried out, and used a "local source"[3] to reveal the role of the illustrious family.

In the introduction, Lynn Perrigo presents a brief history of the original research; nearly ten years, he says, have passed from the time when the young Lynds went to Muncie for their first research. He then explains that they had chosen Muncie because it was a typical midwestern city and that the Lynds' aim was to present a dynamic and functional cross-section of the contemporary life of this specific community, in light of the changes that had taken place there over the preceding thirty-five years. Perrigo notes provocatively that the project was funded by the Rockefellers through the Institute for Social and Religious Research. He then gives some information about Robert Lynd (but none about Helen). His

tone at times becomes ironic as he talks about Robert, and perhaps here
we see a bit of jealousy toward that boy from the Midwest who made it
in the big city and then came back to observe and pass judgment on one
of those cities in Indiana that he had known so well since childhood. Perrigo also observes that *Middletown* was published in 1929, and became a
national best-seller. It was quoted everywhere in the humanities and was
used by publicity agents to promote sales, but not everyone in Middletown had greeted the book with applause. According to Perrigo, many of
Muncie's citizens had the feeling that the city had been tricked and flat-
tered into revealing its secrets, only to then be ridiculed. He handles the
most important criticisms that he thinks can be directed at the Lynds in
three phrases: that the Lynds paid too much attention to economic determinism and minute details and so failed to see the "spirit" of the city; that
they did not pay enough attention to the college; and that they did not
recognize the importance of the X family in the life of the city.

Ten years later, there were therefore two problems that inspired Perrigo
to undertake his work: the changes that had taken place within the various categories, and two areas that were important for the life of the city
and that the Lynds had failed to consider—"ecology" and the Ball family.
With Perrigo's contribution to these questions, we gain a more complete
picture of Muncie at the beginning of the twenties than that which
comes to us solely with *Middletown*.

FROM AREA TO AREA

According to Perrigo, the Lynds overemphasized the getting-a-living aspect of life in Muncie; he has little to add, therefore, to their description,
but he does have a lot to say about the intervening ten years. Perrigo
maintains that the Lynds probably attributed so much importance to this
theme because they believed that it was the most urgent one for the people of Muncie. The poverty of Perrigo's argument is evident here, since
"getting a living" is undoubtedly important for the life of every community, both in times of crisis and in times of prosperity.

Perrigo argues that in 1924 the incessant work of getting a living pro-
ceeded in Middletown, with all its daily difficulties and variables. In 1934
people continued to make a living, but they had to work harder at it. In
Perrigo's view, one of the effects of the Depression can be represented in
this way: while in 1924, forty-three people out of one hundred earned a
living that supported everyone in the city, in 1930 the number of people
employed was thirty-eight per one hundred, in 1932 thirty-four per one
hundred, and again thirty-eight per one hundred in 1934. He further observes that although this phenomenon affected the working class first, it
also had heavy consequences for all workers who were still employed and

for a large portion of business people, since everyone who had an income had to support a greater number of persons, directly or indirectly. In the end, government money lightened this burden, although government intervention was really a mortgage on the future.

The problem of unemployment was so severe, according to Perrigo, that in 1930 one thousand families lived in misery. By 1933 there were two thousand families in that condition, and again in 1934 two thousand families needed unemployment benefits. The number of industries went down from 105 in 1929, to 80 in 1934, and they reduced productivity by 10 percent during that year. The local chamber of commerce encouraged new factories to come to the city, despite the negative experiences mentioned above. Stores managed to maintain their standing, however, and to avoid being bought out.

Two factors were favorable to the life of the city. The first was the growth of the college, the second was the construction of roads radiating out in all directions, facilitating communications, commerce, and the quality of life. Workers in the area became more mobile, and it became necessary for them to have cars, since many commuted to work. As Perrigo rightly points out in this regard, while an intense campaign on safety in the workplace had reduced risks on the job to a minimum, this achievement was counterbalanced by increased danger on the road (in Delaware County there were twenty-five hundred road accidents per year). Businessmen were increasingly using airplanes for their work, and for this reason the aircraft industry had also increased production.

On the whole, Muncie still worked hard to purchase important items like cars. The aspirations of people and their orientation toward consumer goods competed with the idea (and the reality) that people should save money to help with the family budget.

In 1934, as in 1924, workers could be divided between "blue collar" and "white collar," although in the meantime individuals in the two categories were often within the same social class. By 1934 fewer people were buying their first home or changing houses, and fewer were getting married. Household spending was changing in reaction to the Depression with a rediscovery of do-it-yourself activities, from canning to dressmaking. During the same period, employment offices had burgeoned in the city, as had trade schools, in spite of the fact that chance played a large part in determining the type of job any individual obtained.

In 1924 Lynd had found both economic classes (Perrigo did not suggest any "class theory") favorable to a continuation of the laissez-faire system of free competition. But the Depression tested this system severely, as Perrigo notes. Local socialism won some adherents (above all, among working-class people and the unemployed) and a lot of "parlor pinks," or sympathizers who were not ready to act on their political principles. Fortunately for the status quo, business leaders became more tolerant first and then applied their energies to saving the system. And so nothing was done about "socialism," in which, because business improved from 1933 to 1934, people lost interest.

In a certain sense, Robert Lynd's admonition at the end of *Middletown* to "revise our institutions" had had an effect on people. As proof of this, Perrigo summarizes five interviews with residents chosen at random by a local journalist. They were asked if they thought that government regulation was bad for business. All of them answered in the negative, and went on to add that the government's intervention had stimulated the economic and social recovery. When another group of five persons were asked whether communism and fascism were dangerous, they were divided in their responses, one answering yes, another responding evasively, and three answering no. From these responses Perrigo concludes that the general attitude was favorable to capitalism and laissez-faire, while at the same time there were signs of a more liberal mentality in the population.

With regard to "making a home," Perrigo affirms that he does not have many criticisms to make. However, the Lynds did omit discussion about the types of homes and their location in the city, and Perrigo partially fills in this omission in the corresponding section of his own work. He does make two negative observations about the Lynds' work, the first concerning the atmosphere in the home. Lynd had noticed domestic ill feelings and dissatisfaction, particularly among the wives, who were subordinate to their husbands, and his observations contrasted with the stereotypical picture of the "happy home." Perrigo instead believes that this reality actually prevailed in the Middletown of his day. Secondly, without realizing it, he confirms Veblen's hypothesis about conspicuous consumption, but in contrast to Lynd, he applies the idea to Middletown's rich: the upper business class was ostentatious and pretentious, owning imposing mansions and customized automobiles.

In addition, houses now included many more ultramodern appliances than they had ten years earlier, partially thanks to massive publicity campaigns, although the economic crisis at that time meant that people did not use them very much, because of their prohibitive cost. Still focusing on the experience of "home," Perrigo does not touch on the changes taking place within the institution of marriage. He does mention, among other things, that women in Muncie dress more simply because of the recession and that the "new" fashion of smoking is becoming widespread, especially among young men.

Although Perrigo does not question the basic principles that guided the Lynds in connection with their "training the young" category, he explains how and why Middletown's authors underestimated the importance of the college in the life of the city. Indeed, students and teachers affected the artistic and cultural activities in Middletown, both quantitatively and qualitatively. When Lynd chose Muncie (as Perrigo points out, but as Lynd himself admitted), he did not want a significant university presence: this element would have altered the city's "averageness" and as a consequence also its "representativeness."

Perrigo finds Lynd's criticism that the teachers were trained by books and not by experience pointless and false. Perrigo notes that recently many schools have been built and student numbers have increased. The Normal School was changed to a teachers college, and offered diplomas in pedagogy and paramedical training. In 1934 more than one thousand students were enrolled and there were more than one hundred teachers. Education was well thought of in Middletown, including an emphasis on athletics and music. Furthermore, in 1934 the school board planned to emphasize physics, science in general, and the social sciences, although the whole school curriculum was the same mixture of old and new that it had been in 1924. Students enjoyed an unconventional degree of freedom, and tension over grades and promotion had been reduced by the introduction of group work and evaluation. Finally, along the lines suggested by Lynd, there was still a lot to do to eliminate social illiteracy, once basic illiteracy had been eliminated.

Regarding religion, Perrigo says that he does not have many objections to Lynd's work. He even says that Lynd's chapter on religion, like many other chapters of his book, can stimulate an improvement of various institutions—in this case religious institutions. In 1934 the religious practices in Middletown did not seem to have changed much in ten years. There were still forty churches and twenty denominations in the county. The pastors were very active, and often met together to smooth out their rivalries, which existed quite beyond their (rather small) differences of creed. In the intervening years, before the Depression reached its nadir, there had been no important revival, but many churches had been built. Two of the five new churches were especially imposing, with imitation medieval decorations. The new constructions attracted interest and together with the expanded activities of the Sunday schools helped to bring more people to church. After the interruption due to the recession, when everything seemed to stand still, people again seem religiously committed, as they had been in 1924.

In his paper's section "Engaging in Community Activities," Perrigo notes that Lynd looked at such activities (government, health, social assistance, information, and citizen solidarity) with a certain air of indulgence, particularly with regard to local government. In 1934 Middletown was still governed by the antiquated system described by Lynd. There were a mayor, other administrators, and councilmen. The citizens seemed indifferent to questions of government and the local administration's program was vague, in response to their indifference. Then again, Perrigo was not very well informed on the issues, and merely reports on the "Dale case,"[4] which Lynd had discussed in detail as an example of how hard it was for a new democrat to effectively carry out the job of mayor, not to mention the constant pressures he was under from different sides.

A new element in 1934 was the attention paid by the government to health, and the consequent institutionalization of various agencies. Doctors in private practice, in strong competition among each other, used their association to do everything they could to discourage socialized medicine and hospitals, which would take many of their patients away from them. In addition, Middletown had to face the problem of social assistance for the unemployed. In 1934, unemployment assistance was paid to 10 percent of the local population. The community had a heavy burden of social assistance. For example, in 1932 the city spent three hundred thousand dollars in assistance—three times the entire community fund, that is. This had been instituted as a sort of mutual fund: citizens with a good income taxed themselves voluntarily in order to help those less fortunate. Later on the federal government assumed some of the burden, and local tension relaxed. In particular, certain measures were taken in favor of invalids, and experiments were tried out in many different areas. Assistance jobs were established in substitution for unemployment pay. For example, among other help, assistance gardens became important. Here, the poor could work in exchange for certain food stuffs distributed by the city commissary. Private citizens opened dormitories for vagabonds and even the town hall was used as a dormitory for passing vagrants, until a real camp could be opened on the edge of the city. On the whole, in line with Lynd's suggestions, private charity tended to give way to the work of semipublic and government agencies.

In general, information had not changed significantly since 1924. Newspapers were still primarily for amusement and advertising, rather than information in the real sense of the word. In 1934 about one third of the space in local newspapers was dedicated to advertising, and the rest to news and photographs. But a rapid glance reveals that almost all the news came from syndicated agencies and the services were taken whole from other newspapers.

Perrigo notices two opposite tendencies regarding solidarity in the community. On one hand, for example, the social services that had been constructed in response to the economic emergency tended to consolidate; various forms of entertainment improved; and meeting places that catered to a large segment of the population (such as MIRNA, Muncie Independent Retail Merchants Association) were created. On the other hand, the high school was decentralized; local and neighboring athletic teams became rivals; workers had greater lateral mobility (and therefore more competition for jobs), especially with the arrival of laborers from Tennessee and Kentucky; and two new churches on the city's West Side were constructed, which were separate from all the others. Even Lynn Perrigo, the "local source," notices the continual antagonism, which the Lynds emphasized so much, between the principle of solidarity and a tendency toward competition.

Besides a comment to Lynd and some additional information, Perrigo insists on his contribution to two new areas that he identified: the ecology of the city and the domination of the Ball brothers. On both these questions, but especially the second, which gives rise to the more interesting and bitter controversy, we will follow Perrigo's line of argument step by step.

THE ECOLOGY OF THE CITY

According to Perrigo, Lynd dedicated little or no attention to the layout of the city and its social consequences: all Lynd did was to classify the houses into three types. Meanwhile, for Perrigo, the delineation of clearly defined areas of the city constitutes an interesting element for the study of local life and of the transformations taking place as the city grows. He comments that his arguments are not based on a recent, specific collection of data, but on his own personal knowledge of the situation. He believes that it is useful to describe the physical aspects of the city because they are the stage on which the economic and social drama takes place.

At the time he was writing, Muncie had four well-defined zones, organized symmetrically around a town center. First there was downtown, center of commerce and business, constituting the central or main area. Around this zone there was another, mixed area that was partly residential and partly commercial. The third, or residential zone comprised the rest of the city; and the fourth zone was the rural periphery, which was strongly dependent on the city. Each of these zones was subdivided into areas with more or less differentiated functions. The city center contained shops of various kinds, banks, theaters, public offices, the YMCA and the YWCA, and so on.

The area that surrounded the city's "loop" had once been a prosperous residential area. By Perrigo's time, however, it had begun to decline: the houses were not well maintained, and many buildings that had been private residences were being turned into stores, garages, and facilities for light industry. In the eastern part of the same zone there were boardinghouses and rooms for rent. Toward the south, gradually deteriorating, the zone included brothels and a black ghetto.

The large residential area was divided into two segments, with an "urban oasis" in the northwest. People who wanted to be considered respectable went to live there. Single-family houses predominated over semi-detached ones. But there was another, newer oasis near the college, which even rich people who had lived in the fashionable East End were moving to. In Perrigo's time this exodus was not complete, because the older generation was fond of its beautiful homes near the commercial center.

All three zones, including the residential zone, were divided into sections, with the dividing lines formed by train tracks, parks, factories, cemeteries, the river, the golf course, the hospital, and the college.

Muncie's fourth zone extended out from the residential area in all directions. The countryside was visibly influenced by the city, its land being used to produce food (vegetables, milk products, etc.) for the market. On the outskirts of the city, besides suburban residences, there were two airports, a country club, two large industrial plants, cattle pens, quarries, and dumps.

As the city grew—again, according to Perrigo—the social and economic differences between residents in the various areas tended to diminish, and social and economic categories became unstable. This was a transition phase, with the areas near the center becoming increasingly important, to the detriment of those outside the center.

At this point, Perrigo makes an observation that is surprising from a sociological point of view. He believes that the upward and lateral mobility of the residents caused social instability and turbulence. The changes of house and neighborhood among people who moved within their class and those who were on their way up the social and financial ladder created tension and disillusionment for themselves and others.[5] Perrigo blames this phenomenon on the lack of long-term city planning. As we read his analysis of the city's ecology, we have the sense that it was a situation without rules, in which there was freedom for recklessness and conflict that would have long-term effects.

"THE BALL BROTHERS' DEMESNE"

Perrigo's last section deals with the domination of the Ball family, or better, of the Ball brothers. This section, called "The Ball Brothers' Demesne," gave rise to the conflict that I referred to at the beginning of my discussion of the Perrigo manuscript.

Perrigo lists a certain number of "industrial barons," but the Ball brothers were the barons to surpass all barons. The five of them founded a glass factory in Muncie during the phase of rapid expansion in the natural-gas business. They specialized in jars for preserves that were soon being sold everywhere. Success brought them nearly limitless wealth, to the point that the city owed them homage and loyalty. In Perrigo's time, only two of the brothers were still alive, but four of their children and two sons-in-law were operating the business and dividing the wealth among them. They had invested in property, building sites, and buildings to lease to tenant farmers and other citizens. In addition, Perrigo tells us, they had enlisted a following of local "gentry."

More specifically, the Balls' property in Muncie included their glass factory, a paper mill, the Ball department stores, the family homes on Minnetrista Boulevard and in Westwood, the Elliott apartment building, a certain number of houses and plots of land near the college, a cheese factory north of the city, and a lot more, perhaps more than was generally known. Thus they had contributed to the construction of many institutions, including the college. They would buy the land and then donate it to the state and oversee the construction of the main buildings. Near the college was the site of Ball Memorial Hospital (costing the family a million dollars at that time), which Perrigo calls an out-and-out gift to the whole community. The illustrious family also built youth camps, sports facilities, and other public places. The site of the airport was land that the Balls had donated to the city as a municipal field, but when the city failed to develop it, the Balls took it back and built the airport. Two of the five banks that survived the Depression did so thanks to Ball money deposited in them. Without the generosity of the family, not even the churches and schools would have been able to survive.

Perrigo goes on to say that all this socially oriented action would seem to indicate that the Balls were benevolent lords who had worked for, stimulated, and guided the life of the city. Even the effects of the Depression were alleviated by the presence of the Balls and their large glass factory. Indeed, while many other factories had closed down, the revival of homemade preserves produced a boom in the glass industry. Finally, the Balls themselves, with their industry, charity, interest in art, education, and religion, and with their moral virtue to guide them, constituted an inspiring and stimulating example for the whole community. Perrigo notes particularly that the older generation of Balls spent long hours at their desks, and anyone could come to them for advice on the smallest problems.

Perrigo adds, however, that all of this was not without some negative aspects. Above all, the fact that so many groups of people were indebted to the Balls tended to limit freedom and discourage initiative. The very name of the family represented the prevailing economic system, made up of individualism and economic laissez-faire.

Perrigo observes that 10 percent of the workforce in Muncie was employed by the Balls in their different factories and properties. But everyone, Perrigo adds, was dependent on the Balls in one way or another, insofar as the activities that everyone in Muncie participated in were more or less closely tied to the interests of the family.

Besides this limiting effect, there was another negative effect of the family's influence on the city. The institutions built by them had very high operating costs that burdened the community and its citizens by using funds that otherwise would be directed toward humanitarian ends.

Finally, there are the criticisms by the socialists of Muncie, who claimed that the Balls had accumulated their wealth by exploiting the natural resources and the local workforce. They maintained that if the means of production had been controlled and the profits divided, the people themselves would have been able to finance public building, without having to bow to the generosity and largesse of the Balls. At this point, Perrigo asks "But, who among the mass would have taken the initiative?" He imagines that even as simple members of a cooperative company the Balls might have been the ones to coordinate and direct community projects. Or were they and their benevolence simply the products of the system that had allowed them to become rich and therefore powerful?

Above and beyond what might have been, and leaving aside the infantile adulation attributed to the Balls, Perrigo wants to point out that the family knew how to gracefully assume the responsibilities of their wealth, especially compared to others in the same position. He concludes by affirming that an understanding of what these philanthropists, with their widespread local influence, meant to the city offers another key to daily life in Middletown.

THE END OF THE STORY

In his conclusion, Perrigo affirms that *Middletown* is an excellent social analysis and honestly represents the reality of Muncie in 1924. Since Lynd was a cynic, however, and if one wanted to be hypercritical, Perrigo adds, there are several points of contention. Specifically, the young Ph.D. candidate wants to emphasize his three fundamental criticisms of the Lynds' work: their failure to consider the college, the ecology of the city, and the influence of the leading family. He adds that they presumed that a collection of data could really describe a living and moving subject. This generic criticism is the more surprising since it corresponds so little to the spirit that the Lynds brought to their research. Perrigo observes that this criticism can be leveled at the book as a whole, but especially at its treatment of the "spiritual" aspects of community life, which by nature are difficult to pin down to categories of data.

Perrigo notes that although the people resisted change, especially in sensitive areas that touched on their principles, values, and most rooted beliefs, some things had changed for the better in Muncie. There had been improvements particularly in the six areas delineated by the Lynds—getting a living, use of leisure time, training the young, engaging in community activities, and engaging in religious practices. "Someone" (important) in Muncie felt that these improvements had been stimulated by the research of the Lynds, who with their sincerity and honesty had enlarged the understanding of local people and of the whole of contemporary American society.

PERRIGO'S REASONS

The real revelations in the Perrigo paper are those concerning the power of the Ball family. This is the part of the manuscript that makes it worth reading even today. Beyond its intrinsic value, therefore—which is not the object of our discussion—the difficult truth it contains means that it will continue to be read. Is the Perrigo paper the Lynds' original or exclusive source on the X family, or did they already have that information? If so, why hadn't they discussed it? And above all, why did they call Lynn Perrigo simply "a local source," when they could have mentioned him, if not by name, at least in a more specific, complimentary way?

It is a fact that Lynn Perrigo had made a little discovery, however modest, and had also attempted to explain it in a spirit of scientific neutrality. This precious informer had shown them his manuscript; why didn't they compensate him for his generosity? Although Perrigo himself had requested to remain anonymous, the omission might be a convenient alibi for those who stand to profit from it in one way or another. Personally, I find it difficult to establish clarity about this matter on such a flimsy basis; one could make many hypotheses. To cite only one, we could imagine that the Lynds already knew about the X family when they wrote their first book (or at least when they were getting ready to write the second), and so the information from their "local source" was simply supplementary. The absolute secrecy that Perrigo had insisted on prevented them from revealing his name, and according to this hypothesis, what he told them was in any case information they already had.

Not everyone agrees with this interpretation, which puts a lid on controversy and conflict. It is easy to understand that the question is important with reference to Robert Lynd's subsequent career in sociology, and in addition has many different sides. For these reasons, once a kernel of doubt has insinuated itself, I feel that it would be a good idea to present all the arguments of what eventually became a real controversy, until now limited to American scholars specifically interested in the Middletown studies.

Howard Bahr's Turn

Various doubts and perplexities inform the positions assumed by academics regarding what we can now call the Perrigo-Lynd question. Indeed, some academics avoid the issue altogether by exiting through a back door. Bahr makes yet another choice.[6]

Right from the first pages of his article, it becomes clear that Bahr is an expert in the Middletown studies, and knows the places, persons, historical events, and questions of methodology and procedure better than any other specialist. Therefore, we must not underestimate or ignore his opinion on the controversy in question, since if we cannot completely disentangle it, we can at least shed light on what would otherwise have remained in the dark. For this reason, and also because his arguments are so peculiar that even Robert Merton intervened on the question, we will analyze his article on the Perrigo paper carefully.

Bahr enters the discussion in medias res, by noting that the difference between the first and second studies on Middletown is the controversial chapter on the X family. Using the many sources at his disposal, Bahr tells us that Frederick Heimberger, a professor of political science at Ohio State University who had formerly taught at Ball Teachers College in Muncie, wrote to Lynd in 1937 to congratulate him on the accuracy of his 1935 observations. In particular, he was struck by Lynd's knowledge about the influence of the X family. Heimberger carried on a correspondence with Lynd, which Bahr refers to, in which Lynd testifies to the exceptional "local source" behind the famous third chapter of *Middletown in Transition*.[7]

Here Bahr wants to emphasize how much more quickly than in their first study the Lynds managed to get to the heart of many new problems. It is also noted, on the other hand, that they certainly already knew the place well and also what they wanted (Madge 1962). Furthermore, as Bahr himself says, the Lynds' intelligent use of sources recently available to them in 1935, like the Middletown FERA (Federal Emergency Relief Administration), made it easier for them to collect the data that formed the solid empirical basis of their analysis.

Besides those types of data, which formed the appendixes of their book, they also had Lynn Perrigo's paper.[8] This formed an ideal continuation of their first volume, according to Perrigo's explicit intention. In fact, Perrigo had sent a copy to Robert Lynd in the spring of 1935. It is certainly important to note in this regard that Robert received the manuscript just before he went to spend the summer of 1935 in Middletown. It may seem unlikely that that paper, sent to the Lynds so near the time when they undertook their second study, could have had a significant impact on them. It is clear, however, that this paper, like every other local source, could assume an important function for the academic who was returning to the object of his research after a ten-year absence.

In his modest role as school teacher, Perrigo did not have direct contact with the X family, as Bahr admits. However, as he himself tells us, he surely had secondary experience of their local influence.

In 1932, Perrigo resigned from his director's position in the Boy Scouts, and returned to study at Ball Teachers College, where he graduated in 1933. He then went to Boulder, Colorado, where he received his Ph.D. in 1936. He had chosen sociology as a complementary field, and wrote two papers. The first was a study on crime and the environment surrounding it, which was published in *Social Forces*;[9] the second was his dissertation, "Muncie and Middletown," which he never published. According to Bahr, "it constituted one of the documents used by the Lynds when they wrote *Middletown in Transition*."[10]

Perrigo had met the Lynds in 1925 when they were doing the fieldwork for their first book. When the book came out, Perrigo read it and, as he tells us in his autobiography, "While reading it I noted an omission. He [Robert Lynd] had allowed himself to overlook the omnipresent influence of the most important industrial family in the city."[11] While he was away, Perrigo had continued to receive the local newspaper. When he had completed his own paper, he read that the Lynds were planning to return to the city to continue their research. At this point Perrigo sent Lynd a copy of his paper with the explicit request that he not be named. As we have already seen, Perrigo had organized his research around two themes: changes in Muncie since 1924–25, and the accuracy or lack thereof in the Lynds' representation of life in Middletown.

In any case, in his autobiography Perrigo emphasizes his contribution to the Lynds' work as the source for the chapter about the X family. Armed with this retrospective affirmation, Bahr declares, "Despite the inclusion in the manuscript of ample material of the Lynds themselves, Perrigo's influence on Chapter III is obvious."[12] Now Bahr begins his offensive. In an operation that is dubious from the point of view of philology, methodology, and interpretation, Bahr compares a series of excerpts from Perrigo's work and Lynd's, not only from the chapter on the X family, but also on other topics. According to Bahr, the Lynds used their young informer to obtain information about the influence of the radio in Middletown, local politics and government, and the contents of local newspapers. Thus, although it is difficult to prove, Bahr's comparison convinces him of the influence of Perrigo's work on the much more prestigious Lynds.

First Bahr sets up a sort of trial of the Lynds, without ever accusing them directly of plagiarism, but rather of a somewhat cavalier use of the information furnished by Perrigo. Indeed, he feels that Perrigo's influence was sometimes direct, and other times indirect, in the sense that it suggested new opportunities for research to the Lynds and new ways to do it. Toward the end of his article, Bahr completely changes his tone, deemphasizing his earlier points: "Considered in relationship to the whole of *Middletown in Transition*, Perrigo's influence is rather slight."[13] He suggests, however, that academics who want to reconstruct the Lynds' research methods will be faced with the task of clarifying Perrigo's influence on the second book about Middletown. He also explains why, according to him, Perrigo did not influence Lynd's ideas about power in the community very much. In fact, as Bahr later says, Perrigo did not discuss the theoretical aspects of power that interested Lynd. Actually, we could easily add that the young teacher did not have any "theory of power"; nor did he claim to have any. He was useful to the Lynds above all because he could furnish so much information. Although the Lynds surely used other sources, "Without his contribution to *Middletown in Transition* as 'Middletown's' critic, expert and first-hand observer of the changes occurring during the decade, the composition of the book and especially the chapter on the X Family, might well have been very different."[14] In the last sentences of his article, the author seems to want to put things right. Robert Lynd paid Perrigo his private tribute when he wrote on the front page of Perrigo's copy of his book "To Lynn Perrigo who contributed to make this book what it is." Now, according to Bahr, more than forty years after this personal tribute, it is time to make Perrigo's contribution to *Middletown in Transition* publicly known.

From this description, we can note how Bahr changes his tone in the course of this article published in a minor journal. He nevertheless diminishes the originality of the Lynds' work (if not its validity). But who can say how important the people were who inspired, stimulated, or encouraged them to collect information that otherwise they might have missed.

Bahr does not limit himself to accusing the Lynds of shoddy procedures or inadequate methods, or even of sloppy work and omissions. He makes all these accusations and others as a matter of course in his retrospective dissection of the Lynds' work and its inevitable defects. But there is something else at work here. Bahr insinuates that the Lynds' free and profound intuition was channeled, that suggestions helped to fill in lacunae in their work. Unfortunately, the people concerned are no longer here to defend themselves, or just to respond. In any case, the mere act of defending their work would weaken their position. It is an astute move to put someone in the position of having to defend his actions and choices, and of revealing the unconscious inspiration of his work. Politicians know this tactic very well, as do intellectuals.

It is not easy to intervene in such a complicated situation. Only Robert Merton would have the authority to do so effectively.

Robert Merton's Intervention

In 1935, when Robert Lynd went to Middletown for the second time, Merton did not know him yet (in fact, he was in his teens). They met in 1941, four years after the publication of *Middletown in Transition*, when Merton went to Columbia, and liked each other so much that they remained lifelong friends. Merton was close to both the Lynds throughout the various stages (not always fortuitous) of their careers. He was Lynd's advisor in crucial moments, as we can see in the frequent correspondence between the two "Bobs." Merton also corresponded with Helen, especially in her second productive period. In his letters, Merton is always ready to communicate, suggest, and sometimes to push, often returning manuscripts he has read, with notes and suggestions in the margins. This is yet another example of the tireless commitment of that type of intellectual. I was certainly moved to read the correspondence of these men, and at times, I indeed felt that I was violating the privacy of their ideas and intuitions, and more importantly of their sentiments and mutual regard.

Among this material filed under "Perrigo Paper," I came on a real pearl: Merton's indirect testimony about the whole affair, which reveals not only his moral stature, but also his disdain for all forms of waste that sap the difficult task of research. Merton's ten-page letter[15] goes beyond the occasion for which it was written. In fact, it is a sociological text on the best research procedures, and also on interpersonal relations: how to avoid burying the truth beneath a pile of banalities that would only dishonor the scientific community and, especially, the world of sociological research, whose work involves living and therefore vulnerable material.

Ed Lauman, the editor of the *American Journal of Sociology*, had invited Merton to express his opinion on the Perrigo question, brought up by Bahr. Merton's intervention is decisive and very clear. His letter was sent directly to Howard Bahr before it was published, with a copy sent to Ed Lauman. We should note that Merton refers in his criticisms to an earlier version of Bahr's article. In fact, in this final version of the article, Bahr's tone is not so extreme, which we can deduce from Merton's comments, even when he does not quote the article directly. His definition of Bahr's methods as an example of "the Gertrude's syndrome" (explained below) is confirmed by the final version of Bahr's article, which was published in the *Indiana Magazine of History*, a much less prestigious journal than the

American Journal of Sociology. In that sense, it seems that Merton's intervention had produced an effect on both Bahr and his potential readers.

Above all, Merton affirms that there is no doubt about the authenticity of Perrigo's article. Rather, he disagrees for several reasons with the way it is used in relation to *Middletown in Transition*. Then this very articulate letter follows two lines of argument. The first has to do with the tone of Bahr's article, while the second considers the nature of his contribution to sociological analysis. Merton says he does not believe that Bahr meant to accuse the Lynds of plagiarism, yet the tone of the article suggests a conspiracy, beginning with the title "The Perrigo Connection." This phrase, Merton notes, smacks of urgent, murky situations, like "The French Connection" or "The Turkish Connection." Well then, he continues, the Lynds had surely read Perrigo's manuscript, as all the people involved admit publicly and on various occasions (never imagining the fuss that would arise over the question). But this is a far cry from the claim that Perrigo's document hides some unsavory affair. As we already know, Perrigo himself asked the Lynds not to mention his name, not from any modesty, as Merton points out, but for the practical consideration that he might return to work in Muncie. The Lynds, then, deserve only praise for honoring Perrigo's request.

Furthermore, why should we imagine that Perrigo was the Lynds' only source, when witnesses from that period, some of whom are cited by Bahr himself, tell us that many people were in contact with the X family and could have given information even more detailed than Perrigo's? Then again, we need only look at the length of the sections that Perrigo and the Lynds dedicate to the X family and to other topics to see how much material the Lynds added, as well as the quality of their comments—features that are completely lacking in Perrigo's more modest paper. Indeed, a textual comparison proves nothing except that the Lynds analyzed in depth arguments that Perrigo only touched on and that could have been familiar to the Lynds from the network of local informers at their disposal when they started their second work on Middletown.

Merton notes that in Bahr's interpretation, the Lynds' scrupulous observance of Perrigo's request to remain anonymous becomes instead a cautious desire on their part to hide his identity. Bahr does not explain, however, exactly why they would have done this or why he was led to interpret it this way.

Merton then passes on to what he himself called the "non-historicity of Bahr's historical note," and is very convincing regarding both biographical fact and intellectual history. How could anyone ignore the fact that during the ten years in question Robert Lynd had become extremely acute to questions of power, its structure, and the way in which it is exercised? It would be a somewhat hasty deduction to suppose that only Perrigo had become aware of the exercise of power in local communities during those years. For Merton, this is an example of the false idea that when one thing follows another there must necessarily be a cause-effect relationship between them; that, because it was written first, Perrigo's manuscript must have given rise to Lynd's reflections on power. We need only think of Lynd's *Knowledge for What?* to understand how interested he was in the effects of power. The simplistic post hoc argument cannot constitute proof, especially in the presence of many other elements that demonstrate that the two works are very dissimilar. The Depression had come and gone, and Lynd's involvement in progressive politics was well known, as was his daily work in New York, which brought him into contact with thousands of problems every day. But for Bahr these things are not important compared to the influence of the "local source." Therefore, according to Merton, Bahr's reflections regarding the history of ideas and sociology are not historically sound.

Actually, Merton concludes, Bahr's whole position could be reduced to what he calls "the Gertrude's syndrome." The catty allusion is to the response of Hamlet's mother, the queen of Denmark, when she watches the play Hamlet has designed to mirror the murder of his father and the remarriage of his mother to his father's murderer. A queen on stage is reassuring her husband, the king, that she would never marry another man if her first husband died. It is at this point that Gertrude says, "The lady doth protest too much, methinks." She is goaded by her sense of guilt, though no one has accused her; and her speaking of these words suggests the possibility that she is culpable. But in all this, Merton notes, there is a touch of unintentional irony—with paradoxical effects—in the individual's incapacity to see herself in perspective.

Merton's letter, which is more subtle than this summary, concludes by advising Bahr to completely rewrite the text of his article, eliminating the negative insinuations and evaluating the Perrigo paper for its real worth, as a document that might be of some historical interest. Regarding Lynd's famous dedication to Perrigo on his copy of *Middletown in Transition*, Merton adds an effective postscript: What does it prove? In dedications, it is quite common for an author to be generous toward even quite modest contributions, out of enthusiasm for the finally completed work.

CHAPTER 5

Middletown III: The Story Continues

IT IS CERTAINLY TRUE that all "critical" sociological approaches tend to regard society pessimistically and that this pessimism obscures indications of possible changes for the better. From this point of view, social phenomena are defined in terms of "decline," contradiction, monotony, repetition, and lack of innovation. The behavior of individuals is seen in terms of deterioration, obtuseness, acquisitiveness, default, and narrow-mindedness toward others. In this regard, the chapter in the Lynds' second book, "The 'Middletown Spirit,'" is emblematic.

There they give a clear idea of the social profile of the city, its culture, and its stereotypes. Prejudice plays an important part in the lives of the people, along with their desire to "make it" (in terms of wealth, not self-realization). In fact, as we have already seen, the idea of self-fulfillment became an increasingly remote goal, hardly worthy of dedication and sacrifice.

The ability to defer gratification, which was the pioneer virtue par excellence, turned into its opposite: enjoyment of the moment, conspicuous consumption. This meant the end of the traditions that had held the community together and the demise of the individual into the narcissistic consumer. The illusion of consumerism, as the Lynds understood and emphasized, had its origins in a promised happiness that life in the community, which inevitably was too repetitive and limited, could not live up to. In fact, it was an imaginary world that consumerism and its accomplice, advertising, depicted (Campbell 1987). Compared to the new "immorality" based on a kind of infantile regression to the pleasure principle, the sky over Middletown seemed very gray indeed.

That pessimism, however, was not limited to sarcasm or to a desire to make people return to their old values, but was intended to be a denunciation of the defects of society, in order to overcome them. Therefore, change was the lens that filtered the (few) virtues and the (many) defects of the typical American city.

For optimistic sociology, such as we see in Caplow and the third Middletown study, the situation is just the reverse. Reality is seen through rose-colored glasses, contrasts are less vivid, conflicts disappear or seem easy to solve, and institutions "express" the individual, rather than oppressing him or her. Furthermore, whatever its good points, optimism blurs the boundary between wishful thinking and reality. Reality is observed, rather than investigated, and seems made-to-order for the worried reader who is looking for easy answers that won't keep him or her awake at night. The image presented, therefore, is one of stability untouched by change. This image also has the advantage of not broaching anything new and unknown. In the following pages we will be looking at some of the themes typical of this approach.

THE PESSIMISM OF THE LYNDS

Those who idealize the past not only see it though a glass darkly, but also tend to become somewhat bitterly nostalgic for a lost time and place. We have already seen how writers before the Lynds contrasted the undoubted virtues of the small city with its equally undeniable defects. The Lynds were less ideological and more scientific, but nonetheless, they characterized the virtues as having been alive and well in 1890, but no longer so in 1925 (and still less so in 1935).

Even the harsh criticism of Sinclair Lewis, as has been noticed, offered no positive solutions, and could also imply that things were better in the good old days "before the fall." What was needed was a point of view that could break through that dichotomy and delineate it. And yet, with all the differences of their approach, the Lynds also clearly thought that "before" was better than "after," and that mass society had threatened the creative capacities and ability to act of the individual and stifled the good qualities of small communities. People were becoming passive and no longer desired new experiences (Thomas 1923), and their reality consisted in what was easily within reach. The critical attitude of the Lynds is informed by this negative vision of the present, which rather obviously colors the particular situations they examine. And so they see political and economic power as wedded to perverse forces that subjugate the passive and timid elements in society. Their criticism becomes so inclusive that the only hope seems to be a fundamental change in American society. Where the sophisticated humor of Sinclair Lewis was an end in itself, the Lynds' commitment leads them to seek ways out of present problems via recourse to other models of society, which, with their mental inclinations and that particular historical moment, were bound to be versions of planned socialism (Mitchell 1937).

Their pessimism and social criticism predispose them to utopian ideals, the more so given the economic instability at that time, during which the tendency was to look beyond the crisis. In the period between the two world wars, the Lynds witnessed the imperfect attempt of the New Deal to remedy the situation. It seems legitimate to situate the Lynds' social vision in its historical setting, especially if we consider later research on Middletown, which took place in moments of greater social stability, or even recession. It is true, however, that a society is not necessarily more optimistic, integrated, and without conflict, simply because it is more stable. Even small and medium-sized cities suffered traumas and long-term changes that they were not always able to assimilate easily. First of all, anyone who wanted to study Muncie in the 1970's was faced with a city almost twice as big (eighty thousand) as it had been in the 1920's, and much more socially complex. But perhaps this sociological optimism reveals aspects of society that the Lynds neglected, and stops to examine them, acting as an interesting alternative reading typical of recent tendencies in sociology in the United States.

THE OPTIMISM OF CAPLOW AND ASSOCIATES

The most recent sociological study of Middletown examines it not in terms of conflict, but in terms of integration.[1] The new study, which began in 1977, was directed by Professor Theodore Caplow of the University of Virginia. Many of the results are not yet available; in fact, only two volumes have been published to date, one on the family and one on religion.[2] On the other hand, a vast number of articles have been published on many aspects, themes, results, and problems that this latter-day research has revealed. The fidelity to the original study by the Lynds is expressed, above all (and almost exclusively), by taking it as the point of reference against which to measure any changes that have occurred on the stability-growth axis.

The few "novel" elements are based on an initial equivocation. Indeed, the simple fact that they are repeating the Lynds' same questions fifty years later leads the researchers to consider the similarities between the two periods rather than the differences. There is an illusion of something new, but they have their glances fixed firmly on the past. How could they possibly use the same categories and techniques for a reality that has changed so much? When the Lynds arrived in Muncie in the mid-1920's they found a society in the midst of expansion; in the late 1970's, on the other hand, the recession had produced an urban and industrial wasteland: the historical center had been emptied of its significance and earlier function, factories were closed, and workers were unemployed. In addition, the relationship between the local society and the nation as a whole had changed, so that Muncie was no longer as typical as it had been. The "theory of change" proposed by Caplow and his associates merits a separate analysis quite apart from any analysis of the project known as Middletown III.[3]

Fifty years after the Lynds' first research, a group of sociologists arrived in Muncie. They were financed by a grant from the National Science Foundation for half a million dollars. They rented an office near the White River, a beautiful place in town, and began to examine the city. They remained in the community longer than the Lynds had—for about two years, in fact. The heads of research actually remained for only about a year, but they rotated jobs so that they didn't all have to be present at the same time. There were some twenty people in the group, including wives and children, undergraduate and graduate students, secretaries, and interviewers.

But the differences are not limited to the size and composition of the group. The organizational and formal aspects of the team were far from those of the Lynds' adventurous enterprise. When the young couple arrived they were unknown and not particularly experienced, while the recent undertaking was led by three well-known sociologists with a lot of expertise. The three directors were Theodore Caplow, Howard Bahr, and Bruce Chadwick. Caplow was the coordinator and head of the team. He had been a student of Robert Lynd in the late thirties and was Commonwealth Professor at the University of Virginia at the time of the research. He had already written many books and articles, including *The Sociology of Work, Two Against One: Coalitions in Triads*, and *The Academic Market Place*. As I have already mentioned, he was an academic with wide-ranging interests, from theoretical sociology to the sociology of work, social organization, and poverty, and he had worked as a government consultant in the United States and abroad.

The substance of the research was very different from that of the Lynds, as reflected in the complexity of the Middletown III project, and it was destined to leave an indelible sign on the new image of Middletown, U.S.A. Caplow's theoretical position was very different from the Lynds', as is visible in a book that he published just before his research in Muncie, *Toward Social Hope* (1975). There he maintains that human society, and in particular American society, was progressing; that social problems were less serious than they had been and that it was the job of the social sciences to make this known.

Caplow's optimism appears like a mirror image of the pessimism and social criticism of the Lynds (Hoover 1990). Caplow believed, as the Lynds did not, that the system worked in Muncie, and in America, and indeed in general in industrial and postindustrial societies. From the Lynds' theory of conflict, he passes to a theory of social integration, in which the various parts of the social system find their places to form a peaceful whole.

Faithful to the Theme, but Not to Its Meaning

And so, the researchers under Caplow carry forth a very different idea of social change when they come to Middletown, and the spirit of their research goes in a correspondingly different direction than the Lynds'. The research is predicated on a global theoretical model—from which descends, not accidentally, the privileging of "normal" urban areas over "deviant" ones—that tends to see the reality of Muncie as static and reality outside Muncie as dynamic. This style of research assumes that elements of stability are endemic, while change is the result of the infiltration of external tendencies. The researcher does not believe that changes in the society under study take place autonomously, that the society itself is capable of creating social formulas specific to its needs without simply importing them from outside. In addition, in terms of methodology, the researcher simplifies the reality under investigation and renders it homogeneous.

In fact, change in Middletown had come about through the increasing roles played by the federal government, television, immigration, and the growth of the university. But internal contradiction is never really explored, thus making clear that the overall point of view assumed by the researchers was too narrow; they never openly explored what form the community's racial conflict took, or why it never reached the breaking point, since the inequalities between whites and blacks were so extreme and the two communities remained so rigidly segregated. Here, we might also add Appalachian immigrants as a third group, separate from the other two.

Caplow's thoughts on the subject are significant: "Any old Rip Van Winkle from Middletown who woke up during the 1970s after a sleep lasting 50 years would have noted uncountable changes but would not have found any difficulty in finding his way around the city."[4] This doesn't tell us much about any social changes, but only that the city's appearance had changed very little.

CLASSES, LEVELS, AND OTHER
CONSIDERATIONS: THE END OF ANTAGONISMS?

As the reader will remember, when the Lynds returned to Middletown in 1935 to see how the community had survived the Depression, they refined their description of class structure without, however, denying the presence of the famous "watershed" that separated groups and families, divided lives, and determined social destinies—all determined by which side of the line the individual found himself or herself on.

This was the starting point for the team of Middletown III, as they began to explore the questions left unresolved in the first two studies of the American city. One of the first questions they asked was whether differences among the classes had increased in Muncie or not during the fifty years between 1920 and 1970. The team used the data from six ten-year censuses to study job trends. They also compared their own data from 1978 with the Lynds' from 1924 to evaluate changes in the way of life of the two social worlds of Middletown.

First of all, they retained the Lynds' basic distinction between business class and working class (this had been the first use in American sociology of the terms "white collar" and "blue collar"). In the same spirit of "fidelity" they also appropriated the Lynds' classification of families according to the occupation of the male head of the household. Surprisingly, although the Middletown III team had more complete information, which also included data on women's jobs, the results were not very different from those of the earlier work.

The tendencies over a fifty year period seemed clear and analogous to those in other parts of the country. First, there was a slow but constant tendency for the business class to grow—from 29 percent of the population in 1920, to 47 percent in 1970. This change becomes particularly significant if we remember that in the fifty years from 1870 to 1920, the relationship between the business class and the working class had remained fundamentally the same. A second important, if obvious, change was the percentage of workers in the service sector, from 4 percent of the active population in 1920 to 14 percent in 1970. Consequently, there was a change in the relative number of people working with machines and those working with other people. The greatest changes, however, took place at the top of the business class, that is among people in the professions and in the middle range of the service industries.

Caplow's team listed nine job categories to which they allotted points according to a system they had devised. In this way, they were able to measure changes in job inequality, or rather in the way jobs were perceived to be prestigious. The result was that there was a greater discrepancy between the average number of points for business-class jobs and the average number for working-class jobs than there had been fifty years earlier. On the basis of these data, it was clear that the difference was great between the prestige associated with the average white-collar job as opposed to that of the average blue-collar job—and certainly greater in 1977 than it had been in 1924.

TOWARD ONE LIFESTYLE FOR ALL?

However—and this is the surprise Caplow and his associates have in store for us—if we look at the lifestyle of the inhabitants of Middletown, the picture appears a lot more optimistic.

As the Middletown III group points out, most of the Lynds' conclusions about the lifestyles of the different classes in Middletown were based on the interviews they had in 1924 with 122 working-class wives and 44 business-class wives, all with at least one child between six and eighteen years old at home. In order to obtain comparable data, Caplow's group used the same type of sample (systematic-random) for their interviews, though in this case, the interviewers were trained for their work in the field. The interviewers followed the structure used by the Lynds in 1924 as closely as possible. Indeed, most of the questions were formulated in the same words used in the original interviews. It is to the Lynds' credit that fifty-four years after their interviews, the questions were still pertinent and comprehensible. Obviously, many questions that the Lynds did not think of, or which in any case they did not ask, would have been pertinent and useful in the later survey. But, even on a formal level, Caplow chose to remain faithful to his mentor.

The undeniable fragmentariness of the data is compensated by the quality and subtlety of the information obtained, which is far superior— as recent social analysts of Middletown have emphasized—to that generally available to sociologists who try to describe the typical behavior of a bygone era. The information that emerges from the parallel studies (1924 and 1977) concerns the work day, unemployment of the head of the household, the work of married women, the type of dwelling, the relationship between husband and wife, and the role of parents.

While the conditions of daily life have generally improved, the threat of unemployment is still present; though white-collar workers are less vulnerable to it, for blue-collar workers it is a continual menace to which they respond with drastic cuts in basic expenses. Since those who lose their jobs can turn to the more or less generous provisions of the welfare state, their fear and experience of unemployment are less severe than in the past.

The situation regarding the work of married women has improved by 1977, according to Caplow's group. If the husband is unemployed, this is rarely the reason for his wife's entering the work force, and, even when it is the reason, the woman generally continues working even after her husband has returned to work. One unexpected effect of this change is that women of both social classes tend to work.

Compared to the situation in 1924, there has been a significant change of proportion of employed women in the two classes: while the percentage of jobs among working-class women remains the same, the proportion of working women in the business class has increased. In 1924 a working wife was a sure sign of belonging to the working class, but by 1978 it is no longer a characteristic of class. This situation, although not necessarily generalizable to the whole country, is not unique to Middletown.

In the Lynds' time, the distinction between the "rich" who lived in two- or three-story houses in the "fine old neighborhoods" (and this was the local ideal) and the mass of workers was evident. By 1977, an equalizing process has taken place. In the meantime—and this is still true today—the two-story, single-family house no longer represents the ideal, and single-story ranch houses have become the typical family home without distinction of class. Since the type of house (one story or two) is not per se a decisive indicator of class, other external features—lawn, furnishings, and maintenance, for example—are even less characteristic. Caplow's group emphasizes that a progressive egalitarianism has affected even the sort of dwellings (the standard marker of class distinctions) in which people live. Much could be added here, however, about the distinction between comfort and luxury.[5]

The typical working-class marriage of the twenties in Middletown, as described by the Lynds, seemed depressing and frustrating compared to marriage in the seventies. The husbands in those days faced difficulty and frustration in their attempts to maintain their families. The sexual life of the couple was limited by the fear of unwanted pregnancy. Many unplanned children were born, in any case, and parents were exhausted by their efforts to feed and care for their families. They had little energy left over for sexual desire. The situation of the working class in 1924 was distinct from that of the business class even in terms of its private life; in 1977, this distinction is no longer perceptible. Even here, the patterns of life of the two classes seem to resemble each other more.

Both groups of women dedicate less time to domestic work in 1977 than they did in 1924. The picture changes, however, in connection with time spent washing and ironing clothes, which surprisingly increased for both classes, and more so for women in the business class. The fact is, one might add, that the standards of dress and grooming for both men and women are higher than in the earlier period. In everyday life, we can notice many changes, but almost all of them mean a better quality of life. In the first study, one of the class indicators was the presence of paid domestic help. According to the Lynds' research, 90 percent of business-class families had paid, usually part-time, domestic help, while such help was unknown in the working class. In 1978, most business-class families have no paid domestic help, while there is a slight rise of it among traditionally working-class families: yet another instance in which the class differences have apparently nearly disappeared.

You will recall that in the Lynds' study a significant difference was found between the two classes in terms of the amount of time parents were able to dedicate to their children. Things have changed dramatically by 1978, when practically all the mothers spend more than an hour per day with their children (only 7 percent did not) and an even higher percentage of fathers spend some time with them (only 2 percent were totally absent). Not only do the parents spend more time with their children in 1978, they are also more concerned about the social positions their children will eventually occupy, and take a more active role in trying to secure them. Mothers of the earlier generation were resigned, and contemplated their children's futures passively, but by 1978, this attitude has disappeared, and mothers in both classes hope that their children will graduate from college.

We note, however, that whatever the structural appearance in Middletown "fifty years later," the process of social egalitarianism between the classes has not advanced. Caplow's research team fails to connect this very significant fact to the other elements of the social structure. They rather tend to emphasize the progressive assimilation of the different lifestyles of the two classes, and how this blurs the relative importance and prestige of the various professions and occupations. Many aspects of daily life—from houses to clothing, from child care to housework, even values—all seem to indicate a "better" life for both classes and a greater similarity between the classes.

But the researchers themselves do not proceed to suggest that the working class has been completely assimilated in Middletown; that would be equivalent to overlooking the "twofold" social movement that accounts for the increase of business-class women with jobs as well as those who are housewives—or their "double presence," according to Balbo (1981). In fact, due to a complex inversion in lifestyle of women, business-class women in Muncie in the late seventies have more affinities with the routines of working-class women in the twenties than with the routines of the grandmothers within their own class.

These alterations in the lives of women, however, should not authorize the researchers—as indeed happens—to see in them real elements of change leading to the eradication of the notorious watershed between the classes.

"Happy" Family Life

The organization and the structure of the family—notwithstanding the various worries about earning a living and obtaining a respectable status—also seem to assume reassuring characteristics in the eyes of the Middletown III researchers.

In the volume called *Middletown Families*, which is the first to appear of the eventual five volumes, the idea that there has been less social change in Muncie than predicted is once again put forth. This concept will be repeated many times, until it becomes the key to the whole undertaking, informing the conclusions drawn about religion, work and career, and public life.

For Caplow's group, the family constitutes the privileged object of study, and they pay special attention to it in their various investigations of data and in the field. Specifically, they carry out five different analyses of the family: a questionnaire about relations (478 respondents); an intensive study about family dynamics, with 27 interviews; a survey on the role of the family in questions of power and the division of work; a survey of 333 housewives; a questionnaire (with 1,700 respondents) for high school students. The last two surveys repeat the work of the Lynds in the twenties; unfortunately, the data are so incomplete that they are untenable.

Middletown Families does not claim to use innovative research methods, as indeed the researchers make clear about the project as a whole. It was courageous of the team, in any case, to examine these themes over so long a time period, especially since there have been so many studies on the family, many of which have been sadly wanting in intuition or adequate diagnosis. The most original and controversial section of this work on the family concerns the false myth of its decline. This fiction, which has its roots in the past, reiterates several well-known themes: the loss of authority of parents; the generation gap; the isolation of the nuclear family; the weakening of the tie between the family and religion; the large number of women employed outside the home; the increase in divorce.

Middletown Families proposes a positive myth in opposition to this negative one: the same image of the working woman suspended between different worlds portrays her as less subject to stress and more apt to experience tranquillity. The greater tolerance of the population is seen as reducing possible sources of conflict. Old and young are both ready to accept diversity among people, in ideas and traditions; business-class and working-class families are more similar in terms of marriage, the role of parents, and relationships with relatives; even the spheres of male and female activity are drawing closer to each other, and the generation gap is shrinking.

This scenario of the family that finds happiness in its own community (where many young people, besides, choose to remain) must necessarily raise questions for sociologists who study the family, and even for the American reader. And these questions are not only methodological, but interpretive as well: how can we compare two end points, the twenties and the seventies—especially if we hope to learn anything useful—without a profound sense of history? To that purpose, in fact, only biography could fill the void. For example, the students interviewed by the Lynds were senior citizens at the time of Middletown III, and they could have been a precious source of information. But *Middletown Families* does not attempt to create a panel, to connect the two periods through the lives of people, the stories of families and their later generations, and retrospective accounts of the period between the Depression and the Second World War, the postwar period, and the economic recession of the seventies.[6]

An analysis of the survey data produces a photograph of the family in Middletown yesterday and today, but without the historical perspective that would confer meaning on the findings. The unanswered questions about how the present model of family developed from the former—by what turnings, traumas, and transformations—leave most of this process to the rich but risky realm of the imagination.[7]

A Religious Revival?

We have already seen several important differences between the Lynds' style of research and that of Caplow's group; a further difference is their approach to the theme of religion.

While the Lynds believed that religion was becoming a secularized, irrelevant formality for the people of Middletown (to the extent that they feared for its future), in Caplow's volume on religion, *All Faithful People*, the religious institutions of Middletown are seen to be in excellent health. According to the story that book tells, the number of churches had increased steadily since the thirties; church membership and the number of people present at religious services had all increased, as had the contributions of the faithful. The clergy agreed that religion was doing well in Middletown and would continue to do so.

In fact, though, the Lynds and Caplow's group are talking about different things. It had not escaped the Lynds' subtle eye that accompanying a decline in numbers of people present at worship services, the quality of religious life worsened. The churches were becoming increasingly tied to temporal interests, favoring one group over another, rather than pursuing spiritual ends. From the other point of view, the authors of *All Faithful People* never discuss the "meaning" of religion. They admit that sermons tended to be trite homilies, without reference to real social problems, but this does not seem to them motive enough for criticizing religion in Middletown. Their own definition of secularization keeps them from seeing clearly and distinctly what was happening in Muncie in the late seventies. For if we accept their definition of secularization as a social and cultural process tending to lead people away from the influence of religion and religious symbols, Middletown does not seem headed in that direction. But such a restrictive definition does not address the real heart of religious problems, or the nature of religious phenomena.

Although the picture might appear optimistic to the outsider, many citizens of Muncie were not convinced. In fact, Caplow's research shows that a good number of adolescents blamed the churches for being materialistic and neglecting the poor. The Reverend Lawrence Martin, the only nonacademic of the group, wrote the most critical chapter of the volume from his particular inside perspective. In this chapter, inappropriately called "Collaboration Between the Churches of Middletown," Martin points out the rivalry and competition beneath the so-called ecumenical spirit. Furthermore, the constitution of the conservative Association of Pastors prohibits any discussion of social, political, or theological questions.

Even Peter Berger, who in his most recent work has taken a position close to Caplow's, notes an excessive optimism in *All Faithful People*, although he praises the work as a whole. In fact, although he approves of the increase in tolerance and religious participation, this well-known sociologist explicitly says that these elements do not gainsay the theory that society is becoming more secular.[8] The process of secularization, according to Berger, will be better articulated later, taking note of these data on the best-studied community in the world, which are in any case indicative of an important segment of American society. Finally, Berger points out that the results underscore how different in terms of religion American society is from other advanced industrial societies. Americans, even the young, are much more "religious" than western Europeans. And so for the future, we can predict that in places like Middletown, religion will continue to move in the present direction, and will therefore appear archaic, fragmented, and problematic.

As others have pointed out, on the other hand, the persistence of traditional religion, as it appears in Caplow's work, does not preclude transformations of its significance and of the secularization of conscience. Modern times create subtle and often invisible adjustments in religion and culture. The relegation of religion to the private sphere is just one example of how we can only understand religious phenomena by reference to the basic globalizing characteristics of modern society, not by considering them as a purely local and restricted reality.[9]

What American Empire?

The different approaches of the Lynds and Caplow are very evident if we consider the reactions that the people of Middletown had to them. In his preface to *Middletown in Transition*, Robert Lynd noted that the community had disapproved of his interpretation of their reality, and he expressed sorrow that Middletown had stamped him as "cold, analytic, and cynical."

Lynd believed that a community can be analyzed in two ways: we can examine it from the point of view of the community itself, or we can look at the behavior and the institutions of the community as symbols of cultural phenomena, and thereby point out its tensions and gaps. In fact, while the first approach produced a sort of photograph of the status quo, the second interpreted social actions as the egotistical rationalization of specific personal or group interests. Lynd believed that both points of view were needed for a sociological study, although there was the risk, which his own work runs as well, of presenting a twofold picture in which the different perspectives remain separate.[10]

Despite the Lynds' interest in Middletown and their friendship with various people in Muncie, they interpret most of the activities in the city as the expression of an attachment to money: individual and collective actions are seen therefore against the background of a "fixation" with money, which they see as typical of the America of their own time and the future. It is no mere chance, then, that when they found in their second study that this tendency had become even stronger, they paid particular attention to the relative positions of power and the control exercised by the elite's upper classes.

While the Lynds expressed a certain social pessimism and cynicism in their ability to isolate themselves from the environment and the human relations they had established there, Caplow is guilty of excessive optimism. In fact, this helps to explain the positive reaction the local population had to his research (even though, we might add, the evidence for that reaction is limited to three letters to the local paper). Indeed, there was a sort of complicity between the observers and the observed. The Middletown III group congratulated themselves on their harmonious relations with the local population, which they see as signs of agreement with their project: in reality, however, the project never threatened the image the city wanted to project, nor did it question the values or behavior of the inhabitants.

No longer the severe scrutiny of the Lynds, but rather, a bland "participation," and an indulgent observation "from within" the very community observed. Indeed, it has been said,

the Lynds adopted an anthropological perspective in order to view their culture from the outside. "Middletown III," at the opposite pole, represented the height of cultural relativism: members of the tribe indulgently looking on their way of life and congratulating themselves on their fine society without the perspective of the external observer who has experience of other cultures.[11]

The inability of Caplow's group to "interpret phenomena faithfully" is evident in their distance and estrangement from the goals for which the Lynds' practiced social science. In retrospect, the theoretical basis of the Lynds' work is still of interest for sociological studies, even for the work of the Middletown III group. For the Lynds' merit is to have given sociologists, social workers, and lay readers an interpretation of the American microcosm/macrocosm that is completely different from the picture other scientific studies, investigations, reports, and the mass media give us: the criticism, often merciless, of the American "Eden," and of its (almost) infinite ambiguities.

Middletown III presents "new" theories about class that paradoxically echo de Tocqueville's theory about the process of egalitarianism in the creation of mass society (it is no mere coincidence that Caplow's name appears frequently in the *De Tocqueville Review*). However, this modern reuse of his theories ignores the negative aspects of the process that de Tocqueville explicitly mentioned. As so often happens with the ideas of illustrious predecessors, with all due respect Caplow applies them to his own ends.

Theodore Caplow, as we have already seen, with his positive and optimistic point of view, tends to exaggerate the effects of egalitarianism in America; the number and variety of associations represent for him an example of democracy in action, and family ties and the persistence of religion manifest the tried and true values of America.[12]

There is no doubt that de Tocqueville's observations about America are very relevant here. At the beginning of the nineteenth century this French nobleman had already identified the basic contradictions in American democracy (between liberty and equality, for example), and the thousand faces that democracy could assume. Briefly, according to de Tocqueville, the individualism that arises within a "democratic" society gives way to its opposite when citizens form associations and accept the social responsibility that that society imposes on the individual. This happens, however, only as long as social participation implies an advantage for the individual or his or her family. The strength of public institutions in America regulates any tendency toward license, which is the real enemy of democracy in theory and practice: democracy, in other words, contains its own self-correcting mechanism.[13]

In fact, Americans have fought the individualism produced by democracy (today we might say it derives from "mass society") on the very grounds of liberty. The federal system that granted political autonomy to the different states, while it secured their loyalty to the nation, created a rich interdependence among individuals.[14] De Tocqueville's observations are particularly fitting to describe the attitude people had toward politics in the Lynds' Middletown: "It is very unlikely that an individual betrays himself for national affairs; but if a road has to be constructed on his property, all at once he discovers the relationship between public affairs and his private ones and, with no help, finds the link which unites his particular concern with the general one."[15] Furthermore, for de Tocqueville the various associations of community life, clubs, volunteer groups, and similar associations that provide opportunities for public service and recreation—also very important in the life of Middletowners—guarantee and sustain democracy. We have also seen that the widespread struggling for higher social position—attempts to imitate, by any means, the most fortunate members of the community—is as present today as it was yesterday.

De Tocqueville's faith in the ability of America's democracy to overcome its contradictions may be comforting to anyone who wants to maintain the same point of view today, but even in de Tocqueville's work there are other implications. For instance, he points out the restlessness that characterizes America's history and the biographies of individual Americans. Other critics of the "American dream" have echoed his criticism. This restlessness was associated from the start with the strenuous search for material well-being and was combined therefore with a certain anxiety that formed the innovative and competitive character of the young nation.[16]

Those typical American characteristics already seem to represent a contradiction for de Tocqueville, as they do for the Lynds, but not for Caplow. On the one hand, there is the ceaseless search for material well-being and the optimism based on the promise of social mobility; on the other, material and symbolic resources are scarce.[17] Evidently, de Tocqueville perceived the ferment of an imperfect democracy, the structural complexity of which would create the phantom of today's cities, their dispersive reality, in which individuals disappear to give place to inanimate objects.

De Tocqueville's enthusiasm about having the privilege of seeing America in its first stages has translated into postmodern indifference, a "utopia found," an easy trap for people caught in the illusions of postconsumerism. Its signs (they are hardly symbols any longer) therefore became idols against which the subject—accomplice, victim, or stranger?—was finally shattered.[18]

CHAPTER 6

The Nineties in Middletown

The Limits of Change

Going beyond the sociological optimism that distinguished Middletown III, and using a different mental approach and cultural orientation, one sees that an ultimately happy scenario is not possible for Muncie/Middletown. The researchers' good will in pointing out and describing the qualities of Middletown, U.S.A., is not enough to convince us that middle-American cities and the United States are heading toward the best possible organization. American society has grown more complex and this makes us unable to give answers that are certain and unambiguous. We are capable of understanding, however, some of the trends and tendencies that go in the positive direction described by Caplow.

How, then, has "Middletown" changed?

To this comprehensive question, consistent with the true Lynd spirit, we can only answer tentatively. In the Middletown of the nineties there is a series of common phenomena, often found in late modern societies, each with their own local differences but all rooted in the history of American industrialization. For instance, the reduction of people working in blue-collar positions is a recent phenomenon, as is the mobilization of people employed in the more or less "advanced-services sector."[1] The ups and downs on the social ladder are less predictable than in the past, since the idea of "class determination"[2] has become obsolete. The identification of class determinism was the Lynds' great sociological achievement, though at the same time it flawed their interpretation of society, since ethnic determinants and the possibility of relocating within the country greatly reduced the rigidity of traditional social classifications.

Today, the expansion of the college in Muncie is a relevant factor in the city, where many activities revolve around the university. Twenty thousand students in a city of eighty thousand people is no small factor, and it is a factor that certainly has changed the image and reality of Muncie since the period of the Lynds. Ball State University, as the principal institution of the X family, has continued to flourish in accordance with the wishes of the state of Indiana, which is especially proud of the space it has given to education and training.

It can be said that Middletown, in its various transformations and complexities, does not have the characteristics of either a "society" or a "community," because its weaknesses have never really been sufficiently blended with its strengths. The depersonalization of human relations, a strong attachment to individual privacy, together with consumerism and the exclusion of those who are different, constitute the central elements of Middletown.

Different Americas emerge from the empirical field research conducted there: antiabortionist, anti-ERA[3] viewpoints that were anathema even for middle-class New Yorkers. Social conformity, premarital permissiveness, and more or less concealed transgression[4] are the elements that are especially obvious to the European observer, as well as the isolation of those without families—an isolation that, in Middletown as elsewhere, is expressed in various ways. The fact is that people generally do not remain alone, especially those who are still relatively young. Middletown's characteristic of being a "marrying city" has remained constant since the Lynds' time. In fact, Munsonians/Middletowners still overwhelmingly prefer marriage (even serial) and family to any other way of organizing their private lives.

Churches, for their part, continue to offer socialization without integration, since they are, in fact, divided by social and professional class, and ethnicity: blacks attend the Baptist church in the same way that intellectuals, except for a few Presbyterians and agnostics, tend to belong to the Unitarian church. This latter is a "church" without a dogma or beliefs, or any theology. But churches in small and medium-sized cities of the United States become places where debates are held, where people meet each other or hold conferences that later form the basis of lively and competent debate. I personally attended a few conferences in the local Unitarian church. Once the conference included a performance by a famous woman leader of the New Age movement. The Unitarian church is also the place where many single people converge because of its broad views and the possibilities there for socializing.

For a moment, let us reverse Mary Douglas's expression according to which people think in line with their institutions.[5] The symbolic basis of life for the inhabitants of Middletown is informed by their attention to money and technology. This attention in turn creates their identity and sense of belonging. The great variety of people who form this "melting pot" do not create a variegated society, however, especially in Middletown where money is venerated as a sign of success and divine blessing.

In fact—and this is true throughout America—the metaphor of the melting pot is losing its hold (Ferrarotti 1991). Although individuals live in their separate enclaves, they are brought together by a double myth: personal success and the desire for integration in their community.[6] And this is true in both great cities and provincial towns.[7]

As the reader will remember, the Lynds supposed that their original investigation would satisfy a requirement for universality, while at the same time they knew that the specific focus would inevitably limit the application of their findings. This tension between the specifics of the investigation and the ideal of universality was—and still is—stimulating, although it hides something else: that the end of community as such is related to the development of new types of social and human relationships that we can observe and understand. For example, the crisis of capitalism and its ideological apparatus can be observed through the dynamics of single individuals in their different groupings and biographies. One sees this, in other words, by taking into account the connection between general social transformation and the changes that occur in everyday life.

The story of Middletown—to which there is no guaranteed happy ending—unfolds through this "return to the individual," which is one of the characteristics of the Lynds' inquiry and style of interpretation. And the continuing uneasy fascination for the Lynds' work and the difficult reality of Middletown itself stems from the uncertainty of this story's ending.

In this book I have said quite a lot about the Lynds as authors and as committed intellectuals, and somewhat less about later, less successful research done in Middletown. But I have said much less about Middletown today. As Stroppa points out, the Lynds wanted to describe a local world that has partly disappeared, more or less painlessly and with differing social and human costs.[8] In the last analysis, notwithstanding the time that has passed since the Lynds' studies and the changes that have taken place, Middletown remains a pocket of provincial America, with all its contradictions and transformations. If anything, like the rest of America Middletown is undergoing a process of "normalization." The few hippies who passed through have now disappeared, while the "freaks," as always, seem more and more bizarre as their surroundings become ever more mundane.[9]

We European scholars need to look at these phenomena without our European points of reference; although Italian or French urban realities may seem similar, there are in fact no points of contact, either symbolically or materially.[10]

Helen Lynd often said that while she herself could not have lived permanently in Middletown, Robert could have.[11] In fact, neither they nor the others who did research there actually lived for very long in Muncie. They all returned to where they normally worked and lived, their everyday reality, although perhaps they felt disoriented at first and found it difficult to re-adapt. Then, once they had made the break, they were left with a nostalgia that idealized their experiences and colored their biographies, but that also alerted them to their works' incompleteness.

The Confusion of Values

It is perhaps worthwhile to return to a central issue that has become the intellectual property of all sociologists: to that starting point, "American values," that was for the Lynds, and still is for many sociologists, suspended somewhere between acquisitiveness and materialism.

Conceptual and interpretative criteria still develop within the context of sociological theory, in particular, when we refer to the relationship between community and society as worlds of meaning. This is how the discourse about values becomes relevant.

Following Dewey, Bender has recently acknowledged that modernization does not necessarily preclude "community" as a form of relationship between individuals. People living in large groups still need community, even though the numbers of other people involved guarantee that it will assume a different, though perhaps better form. Modern life, confronted by realities and contexts much vaster than before, frees individuals from the constraint of small traditional cities, where people met face to face but also were subject to intellectual stagnation. Now, however, local communities and cosmopolitan societies in their creative gamble produce the basis for a more effective and intelligent democracy—if we are able to manage this complex process, that is.

In this respect, community and society seem to be both distinct and interrelated in all cultures. The anthropologist Redfield cited Lynd's Muncie of the twenties when he wrote *The Little Community* in 1955. Comparing his study of Chan Kom, a Mexican village, with the data on Middletown, he observed that urban and traditional customs were present in both places. It was a matter of grasping the kinds of interpretation in the two environments. As Redfield says, those who analyze community need two different lenses to observe a composite reality. In this sense, Middletown is seen as the coming together of two opposite ways of living, thinking, and feeling that are analyzed simultaneously from two points of view: both the isolated, homogeneous, sacred, and personal community, and the heterogeneous, secular, and impersonal community that we find in the city. From this perspective, we cannot analyze the community as though it were merely a specific space, or simply the basis for historical change. It is instead a fundamental and durable form of social interaction. For this reason, there is no sequential development from community to society, as hypothesized by Toennies and by Louis Wirth of the Chicago School, but rather the simultaneous intertwining of the two points of view in each individual. Furthermore, sociological analysis is interested in the interaction of different types of lives. The sociologist cannot merely affirm that there is a continuum; his or her job is much more complex. He or she has to find out which of these two models of human interaction is stronger at any given moment.

Studies on the community seem ready for a sort of renaissance, exactly because they are able to bring to the fore multiple levels of significance. In particular, the study of social change, which varies so greatly from place to place, even within the same country, can be studied best in small areas. Then again, as regards methodology, locality studies manage to combine standard techniques with the deep analysis of biography and history. From this point of view, we can dust off and successfully use the Lynds' technique of participant observation. By combining different forms of observation, the sociologist who studies the community has an advantage, because he or she has the immediate satisfaction of understanding the situations and relations observed, and also works on another level to explain their deep meaning.

In addition, the sociologist carries out a demystification of social reality and works, by using the various methods at his or her disposal, to establish a balance between the specific phenomena observed and the general principles that can be derived from them—between data and theory, in other words. We find all these elements in the classic studies on Middletown, even though we may notice some understandable omissions. If we continue in the direction indicated by the two young sociologists in the twenties and thirties, sociology can learn much about the difficult and composite changes in our own postindustrial society.

The Lynds recognized in their time that the community was losing its coherence (without disappearing, however), but they also paid attention to the new social forms that were appearing. The touch of nostalgia that they express in their first study was perhaps due to a certain clash in Muncie between recently imported urban elements and local traditions.

Muncie took on this hybrid form that did not create a mixture of the local culture and the greater society, but kept them distinct and contradictory. The city remained suspended between the languid traditions of the past and the uncertainty of all that was "modern": it was like an individual suddenly passing from the simplicity of childhood to the bodily decrepitude of old age, without going through any solid experience of adulthood. We can use this biographical metaphor to explain the lack of cumulative (historical) experience in a whole continent. And thus, we are inclined to read de Tocqueville from a pessimistic, rather than from an optimistic point of view. Indeed, the latest "modernization" of Muncie/Middletown (the late seventies to the nineties) strikes us as a sort of disenchantment.

As I have often said in this book, the Lynds, like Dewey, were convinced that the process of modernization was not incompatible with a strong sense of values. For them, the persistence of traditional values without progress would have been equivalent to a continuation of the mere empty vestiges of the past, while progress toward the modern world unaccompanied by values would have meant a civilization without a soul.

From this point of view, the symbolic roof over Middletown seems somewhat lower—as it already did in the chapter on the "spirit" of the city, in the Lynds' second study. Today, a sort of immobility seems to characterize the social destiny and personal lives of the people in Middletown, apart from their dissatisfactions, which will probably never rise to the level of conflict. But without open conflict, agitation remains smoldering beneath the embers, only to flare up into personal misdemeanors.

Even the "typical" person that one meets in Muncie is particular, neither the westerner known from the movies and literature (the lone hero who is both eternal youth and strong man, generous and violent, as required by life on the frontier), nor the cosmopolitan, distracted, slightly dandyish eastern (and, today, also the urbanized western) careerist. The Midwest is, of course, geographically (more or less) central, and midwesterners tend to be closed toward people who are "different," and like easterners they are acquisitive. At the same time, midwesterners are proud to represent the good American white, Anglo-Saxon Protestant who remains tied to the values of an agricultural society, even in the postindustrial world of today. Many midwestern families (in Minnesota and Wisconsin, for example) originated in northern Europe, and they have had little contact with the ethnic diversity of big cities.

Society's present tendency toward private concerns goes in the opposite direction from the one the Lynds hoped the city, and the country as a whole, would take. There is no public response to social problems today in Middletown, and local politics is bogged down in petty quarrels, while the great national problems are forgotten. Only a small group of intellectuals associated with the college is active in the fight for civil rights. But even the members of this small group avoid direct involvement in local or national politics. Politics is left to the professional politicians, as indeed it was in the Lynds' time, with the exception of the odd young businessman.

Middletown is a corner of America like any other, which has undergone a massive transformation from the industrial town of the past to a place where most jobs today are in the service sector. For all that, it is a sleepy place, which still retains vestiges of material well-being. Its normality is recompensed; it is proud of itself and of still representing some part of the industrialized north of the United States.

As you drive into Muncie/Middletown, the road signs proudly announce that you are entering AMERICA'S HOMETOWN.

Reference Matter

1. Helen M. Lynd, "Middletown" (speech delivered when she accepted the American Sociological Association's Community Section Award for her work on the Middletown studies, August 30, 1980), p. 1. I was then chair of this awards committee. When Ms. Lynd finished reading her memoir she gave it to me, and I filed it in my Middletown folder. I retrieved it when I was asked to write this Foreword and have since submitted the original to the Center for Middletown Studies.

2. Ibid., 5.

CHAPTER 1. ROBERT J. LYND: PORTRAIT OF AN AUTHOR

1. See Nisbet (1981: 72).

2. See R. S. Lynd (1922a and 1922b); and Staughton Lynd, "The Elk Basin Experience," *Journal of the History of Sociology.*

3. H. M. Lynd (1983).

4. Ibid.: 34–40.

5. See Bourdieu, Chamboredon, and Passeron (1968).

6. According to Ogburn's theory of "cultural lag" in modern society (1922), basic changes of material culture are faster then changes of nonmaterial culture. This means that modifications of technology are not followed by modifications of cultural elements like values, ideas, institutions. For Ogburn, the latter should inform, regulate, and control the use of material culture.

7. Also see W. I. Thomas (1927: 4ff).

8. In the words of the author, "Everywhere in Middletown one sees these small businessmen looking out at social change with the personal resentment of one who by long defensive training asks first of every innovation, 'What will it do for (or to) me?' The resulting tendency is to stress the negative aspects of new proposals and for local opinion to dwell upon and to crystallize around extremes of possible abuse which might occur. The tendency noted is not so much a com-

mentary upon the type of people Middletown businessmen are as upon the kind of culture in which they have grown up and to which they must largely conform if they are to survive. They live in a culture built around competition, the private acquisition of property, and the necessity for eternal vigilance in holding on to what one has. In such an exposed situation, rife with threats and occasions for personal tension, human beings tend to react primitively in the direction of warding off threats and seeking to conserve whatever stability they have personally been able to wrest from their environment.

Across the railroad tracks from this world of businessmen is the other world of wage earners—constituting a majority of the city's population, nurtured largely in the same habits of thought as the North Side, but with less coherence, leadership, and morale" (Lynd and Lynd 1937: 24–25).

9. Regarding possible sources of the Lynds' new focus on the Ball brothers, see Perrigo (1935).

10. See Madge (1962: 219–20) regarding Helen Lynd's switch to sociology psychology from sociology. Also see Caccamo (1996).

11. In Horkheimer's words:

Today even the most qualified scholars confuse thinking with planning. Disgusted by social injustice and hypocrisy which is often clothed in the garb of religion, they wish to marry ideology to reality; or, as they prefer to put it, help reality become more responsive to mankind's heart's desires by applying technical methods to religion. Following the trail blazed by Comte, they hope to invent a new social catechism.

Horkheimer cites a portion of Lynd's *Knowledge for What?* on the moral responsibility of science. He then comments: "To all appearances, Lynd regards religion in more or less the same way he regards the social sciences themselves; whose survival will depend, in his view, on the capability or incapability of demonstrating itself useful to mankind in his life's struggle. Religion becomes pragmatic." Horkheimer (1947: 108).

12. See Engler (1979–80: 121–80) regarding Lynd's methodological reflections.

CHAPTER 2. MIDDLETOWN I: ECLIPSE OF THE COMMUNITY

1. Lynd referred to the depiction of the "midwestern character" he found in Dewey (1922).

2. Parrington 1954: 476.   3. Ibid.: 479.
4. See Lynd and Lynd (1929: 5).   5. See Wilson (1974: 11).
6. Curti (1950).   7. See Toennies (1957).
8. Ibid.   9. Giannotti 1977: 527.
10. Ibid.: 535–36.   11. Toennies 1957: 46.
12. Treves 1963: xix.   13. Ibid.
14. Nisbet 1969: 30.

15. See Mills (1953). Like the Lynds, Mills was representative of "critical sociologists" at that time.

16. Nisbet 1969: 105.   17. See Plant (1974).

18. See Bender (1978).

19. See Chase (1931).

20. See Mannheim (1953).

21. Izzo 1991: 99.

22. See Rossi (1963) and Lingeman (1980).

23. See Stein (1960: 109).

24. Ibid.: 112.

25. see H. M. Lynd (1983).

26. See Park (1924: 264–65).

27. See Wilson (1974).

28. H. M. Lynd 1983: 32–33.

29. Ibid.: 29.

30. Ibid.: 37.

31. Ibid.

32. Ibid.: 38.

33. See Rivers (1906) and Wissler (1923).

34. Lynd and Lynd 1929: 4.

35. Ibid.: 6.

36. Ibid.: 505.

37. Ibid.: 506.

38. Ibid.

39. Ibid.: 507.

40. See Etzkowitz (1979–80).

41. Lynd and Lynd 1929: 21.

42. Ibid.: 22.

43. Ibid., note 3.

44. Ibid., note 2.

45. Ibid.: 496–97.

46. Ibid.: 23.

47. Cavalli 1970a: 420.

48. Lynd and Lynd 1929: 481–82, 484.

49. Cavalli 1970a: 420.

50. Ibid.: 421.

51. Lynd and Lynd 1929: 39.

52. Ibid.: 246.

53. Ibid.: 225.

54. Ibid.: 225–26.

55. Ibid.: 246.

56. Ibid.: 271.

57. See Goist (1977).

58. Lynd and Lynd 1929: 502.

CHAPTER 3. MIDDLETOWN II: WHAT TRANSITION?

1. In the Lynds' words, "It is the constant lament of the social sciences that the subjects of their study can never be analyzed under exact experimental conditions. There is no escape from this, but it becomes the more important to exploit as far as possible anything approaching an experimental situation where it presents itself. Here is an American city which had been the subject of eighteen months of close study in 1924–25. During the following decade the conditions of its existence had been unexpectedly altered in a way which affected every aspect of its life. Its growing population had been tossed from prosperity beyond any experienced prior to 1925 to an equally unprecedented depression. The opportunity thus presented to analyze its life under the stress of specific interrupting stimuli, whose course can be traced, offered something analogous to an experimental situation" (Lynd and Lynd 1937: 3–4).

2. For example: "The returning visitor does not even rub his eyes, so familiar are the old civic issues: some people still want the railroad tracks that bisect the city elevated to remove the grade crossings, and the railroads and other people who own factories with sidings on this railroad continue to block the move; there is still trouble over the tendency of the impartial jury wheel to turn out the names of the needy favorites of those in power; the nine city fathers, balloting on a tight issue, could still in June, 1935, when they voted on a new member of the school board, perform the miracle of finding ten votes in the box; Middletown wives still complain of the 'smoke nuisance,' though the depression has softened

somewhat this chronic complaint, as there is at the moment a very lenient attitude toward factories able to operate at all, smoke or no smoke; the city health officer still tries to bring local milk up to the standards legally required by the State Board of Health, and the council still resists the move; the headlines still carry such news as 'Mayor Indicted by Federal Grand Jury'; North Side candidates still run as ardent partisans of the South Side; the old battle to construct a sewage-disposal plant that will take the stench out of the river and 'make the White River white' still drags along, to the gloomy prediction of the press that 'it will probably not be solved until the year 2000.'

Here too, awaiting the observer is the same type of person serving as city official, the man whom the inner business control group ignore economically and socially and use politically. The newly elected mayor in 1935 was the man whose last term as mayor had been terminated fifteen years before by a sentence to the Federal penitentiary for fraud, and with his duties as mayor he still carries on his private medical practice, with the aid of advertisements in the press.

And again one meets in the homes, business offices, and civic clubs the same blend of alternating exasperation and cynical apathy regarding the local civic administration that pervaded Middletown in 1924–25. And back of it all is the constant play of interested 'deals' whereby the controls of the local *Realpolitik* are made to work in the interest of private interests or private interpretations of the public interest" (Ibid.: 320–21).

3. It had yet to be seen whether, "in other words, the boom of the late 1920s had been essentially but a further extension of the old midland American gospel of 'progress,' and the succeeding depression, however drastically felt at the moment, little more than an external depression in a ball ready to spring back the moment the outside pressure was released . . . the decade 1925–35 might not have affected all elements of the city alike. Thus, for instance, the impact of these changing years upon business class and upon working class might conceivably have been different; or some sectors of living might have changed radically and permanently for all the people in Middletown, while other areas of living remained much as they were in 1925" (Ibid.: 5–6).

4. On the stages of putting together *Middletown in* Transition, see Cavalli (1970a: 5).

5. Ibid.: 10.

6. About the influence of the New Deal on American attitudes, see Dahrendorf (1967).

7. Cavalli 1970a: 433.

8. Etzkowitz (1979–80).

9. See Ferrarotti (1989) regarding the methodological development in Lynd's work from *Middletown in Transition* to *Knowledge for What?*

10. About the Lynds' decision-making process toward organization of the second research, see H. M. Lynd (1983).

11. On the influence of the automobile on American consciousness, see Flink (1972).

12. Lynd and Lynd 1937: 4.

13. In the words of the Lynds, "The brevity of the field work made the use of

refined research techniques and measurements impossible. Existing records of all kinds were combed, scores of interviews both formal and informal were made and recorded, the research assistants lived in homes scattered throughout the city and participated in a variety of the normal social affairs of the city; and newspaper files from January, 1929, through November, 1936, have been searched systematically, with a coverage of six to twelve months in each year. Since the field work came to an end, any additional data have been secured from national and local sources, again with the assistance of Middletown people" (Ibid.: 5).

14. See Bell (1974) regarding the "evident and explicit" quality of the Lynds' second research.

15. See Stein (1960: 108–109) regarding the Lynds' interpretation being limited because of its local emphasis.

16. See Thomas (1928).

17. See Marcuse (1968).

18. More specifically: "But, averse as Middletown is to any sort of dictatorial control, what its business leaders want even more than political democracy is what they regard as conditions essential to their resumption of money-making. And those who do the more conspicuous money-making are probably prepared to yield a good many other things to the kind of regime that will flash for them the green 'Go' light. These men recognize the power of the strong man, the man with power, and being successful in business is one long apprenticeship at adjusting to stronger men than oneself. They do not fear such a man, providing he is on their side. . . . If, when, and as the right strong man emerges—if he can emerge in a country as geographically diffuse as the United States—one wonders if Middletown's response from both business class and working class will not be positive and favorable. For unless there is a sharp rise in working-class solidarity in the interim, this Middletown working class, nurtured on business-class symbols, and despite its rebellious Roosevelt vote in 1936, may be expected to follow patiently and even optimistically any bright flag a middle-class strong man waves. . . . It is at least possible that this opposition in the name of traditional laissez-faire freedom would recede in the face of a seizure of power carefully engineered as *by* the business class and *for* the business class and publicized in the name of Americanism" (Lynd and Lynd 1937: 505, 509–510).

19. On Bourke-White's depiction of Middletown, see Goldberg (1986: 188).

20. See Cavalli (1970a: 437–38) regarding this attempt.

21. The authors also comment: "These two elements in Group 2 constitute socially a unity but, in their economic interests, often represent somewhat divergent elements; for while all of Group 2 tends to follow the lead of the upper class (Group 1 above), the salaried dependents of Group 1 do so unreservedly, while the "old" middle class of native small manufacturers, professional people, and substantial retailers seeks occasionally to assert its independent identity as the "real" Middletown, and it even at times offers resistance of an overt or passive sort to occasional moves by the dominant big-business interests that "run" the Chamber of Commerce. On important matters, however, this native "old" middle-class element may usually be counted upon to huddle close toward Group 1. In critical decisions Groups 1 and 2 still tend to constitute in Middletown a single group" (Lynd and Lynd 1937: 459–60).

22. Madge 1962; Caplow 1979; Vidich, Bensman, and Stein 1964.

23. Cavalli 1974.

24. Ibid.: 467. The Lynds also state: "And, in order to renew the semblance of unity in such a city of many human units tied to local residence chiefly by the accident of job tenure, those at the top who want united action must increasingly invoke emotional symbols of a non-selective sort by which masses can be swayed. And, with the fiber of community life rendered flabby by the presence of many untied persons, the ideologies and symbols that move the community tend to be generated at the top and to be imposed on those below, rather than rising spontaneously from the soil of community life."

25. Ibid.: 467–68. And: "One insensibly becomes a citizen of a wider world as a larger city tends to develop a more metropolitan emphasis in its press, as its stores become more sensitive to the 'latest New York styles,' and as better-known speakers can be imported for civic clubs, and so on. One may hazard again the guess that this trend toward less localism tends to affect upper-income folkways somewhat more markedly than those of the lower-income people—though differences in this respect based upon income are probably less today than ever before, due to the heavily democratic character of the movies, radio, periodicals and other mass media which import the outside world." The Lynds then continue with Veblen's thesis about "the paramount importance of 'conspicuous consumption' as an identifying device in a community grown too big for more subtle means of appraisal."

26. Ibid.: 71.

27. The Lynds continue: "The ladder has lost some lower rungs, with the disappearance of apprenticeship and the large measure of blurring of the distinction between unskilled and skilled labor.

The step up to the first rung where the foremen stand appears to be getting higher and therefore harder for the mass on the floor to make.

Above the foreman's rung the whole aspect of the ladder has changed in three notable respects since 1890 and especially since the World War:

It is more difficult for the enterprising mechanic to find an alternative way up the ladder by launching out with a plant of his own in competition with the existing productive structure of large-unit plants.

Above the foreman's rung, the ladder is ceasing to be one ladder: there have virtually ceased to be rungs between the foreman and a higher section of the ladder beyond his reach where an entirely new set of personnel usually not recruited from working-class personnel begins.

And, finally, the ladder has lengthened with the relative increase of 'absentee ownership' of local plants as units of national corporations, and the increasing absorption of formerly independent local manufacturers into the payrolls of these national corporations" (Ibid.).

28. The Lynds state in this regard: "Our American culture has founded its exuberant boast of a classless society upon the two facts of universal suffrage and of vertical mobility up the pecuniary ladder. In the past reality and the alleged permanent continuance of this universally accessible ladder lies the popular justification of the reigning laissez-faire philosophy—as regards the present predatory practices

of business enterprise, the pattern of uneven distribution of the national income, and the virtue of self-help in contrast to the alleged 'immorality' of many types of social legislation, from public 'doles' and unemployment insurance to old-age security. As symbol and reality draw thus apart, the scene would seem to be set for the emergence of class consciousness and possible eventual conflict. But dreams, when they express urgent hopes and are heavily supported by the agencies of public opinion, have a habit of living on in long diminuendo into an era bristling with palpably contradictory realities. Middletown labor is not markedly aware of any crystallizing class status or of the tenuous basis for its dreams. So it tends to be oblivious of the apparently fundamental alterations in the American ladder of opportunity; it continues, for the most part, to view its disabilities as unfortunate temporary set-backs in a naturally ordained forward movement" (Ibid.: 72).

29. According to Jensen (1979).

30. Thernstrom 1964.

31. The Lynds affirm: "Middletown's small-city culture is set up to provide for the more urgent needs of the commoner personality types and functions; and it presents a deterring conservative front to the type of woman who would explore unusual vocational opportunities. The small community tends to be a place of usual personalities, usual jobs, usual recreations. Many of the odd personalities—the political or economic radical, the artistic individual, the person with a flair for the unusual—migrate to larger cities where the cultural pattern is less rigid, the diversity of personal interests and types wider, and the chance to develop selective personal associations or vocational clienteles is correspondingly greater. Those unsatisfied souls who remain in Middletown tend often to carry on difficult lives of outward conformity and unhappy underlying rebellion" (Lynd and Lynd 1937: 64).

32. Ibid.: 147.

33. Ibid.: 148. The Lynds explain it like this: "In most primitive societies one ordinarily has neither status nor the means of day-by-day sustenance and human association unless one belongs to a family. At the other extreme, in a highly urbanized place such as the metropolitan city, status depends not so much upon membership in a family as upon what one can buy, and there have developed in recent decades a variety and completeness of commercial services—providing food, shelter, care of clothes, companionship, recreation, and other needs—which render marriage an optional choice to a probably unprecedented degree. For the personality that fails to find a satisfactory mate of the other sex or that elects personal comfort outside of family life, the modern metropolitan city offers many opportunities and few inescapable penalties. In between these two extremes lies a city like Middletown" (Ibid.).

34. Ibid.: 203.

35. Ibid.: 215.

36. Ibid.: 225.

37. "According to the early American tradition the schools served as an extension and transmitter of the values upon which parents, teachers, religious and civic leaders were in substantial agreement. But during recent decades—as home, church, and community have each become in themselves areas of confused alternatives, and education has developed a professional point of view of its own, *of* the

culture, but also somewhat *over against* the culture—it is not surprising that Middletown's schools have been becoming by quiet stages increasingly an area of conflict, an exposed focus of opposing trends in other social institutions, whose contradictions become more acute and threatening to Middletown as the shape and import of incipient immediate conflicts are magnified on the screen of the next generation" (Ibid.: 231–32).

38. On alcohol-drinking culture in small American towns, see Bogg and Caccamo (1990).

39. Ibid.: 372.

40. Ibid.: 93.

41. Ibid.: 74; 74, note 2; 74–75.

42. See Barnard and Carmony (1954); F. C. Ball (1937); and Moxley L. Ball (1986).

43. Lynd and Lynd 1937: 75.

44. And they add: "The power of this family has become so great as to differentiate the city today somewhat from cities with a more diffuse type of control. If, however, one views the Middletown pattern as simply concentrating and personalizing the type of control which control of capital gives to the business group in our culture, the Middletown situation may be viewed as epitomizing the American business-class control system. It may even foreshadow a pattern which may become increasingly prevalent in the future as the American propertied class strives to preserve its controls" (Ibid.: 77).

45. Ibid.: 93.

46. Ibid.: 94.

47. See Sigfried (1940). This essay is very useful for its French perspective on Middletown II.

48. See Stein (1960: 312–13).   49. Lynd and Lynd 1937: 402.

50. Ibid.: 421.   51. Ibid.: 427.

52. Ibid.: 471. The Lynds also comment that Middletown has become such as it is because of a number of reasons: "from its very location in a northern climate where a long winter follows the season of crops and the earth's yield varies so that cautious husbanding of its output has until recent generations been necessary; from the Christian eschatology; from the stern Puritan emphasis upon 'developing' one's character through careful, thrifty stewardship; from the spirit of private capitalism with its stamp of authority upon individualism and an endlessly growing acquisitiveness; from the frontier tradition under which one was in process of building, ever building, tomorrow out of a crude present; from the validating nineteenth-century doctrine of evolution; and, more recently, from the hypnotizing promise of more and more things tomorrow which its machine technologies and rising standard of living offer" (Ibid.: 469).

CHAPTER 4. MUNCIE AND MIDDLETOWN: THE CONTROVERSY ABOUT THE PERRIGO CASE

1. See Kolko (1962).

2. Lynd and Lynd 1937: 74; 74, note 2.

3. Ibid.

4. See Chapter 3 of this book.

5. See Goldthorpe et al. (1973) regarding the link between the working class and affluent society.

6. Bahr 1982.

7. See Frederick Heimberger to Robert S. Lynd, 16 June 1937, Robert S. Lynd and Helen M. Lynd Papers, Manuscripts Division, Library of Congress.

8. Perrigo 1973: 157–58.   9. Perrigo 1938.

10. Bahr 1982: 7.   11. Perrigo 1973: 204.

12. Bahr 1982: 20–21.   13. Ibid.

14. Ibid.

15. The copy of the letter from Robert Merton to Howard Bahr is dated 30 March 1980.

CHAPTER 5. MIDDLETOWN III: THE STORY CONTINUES

1. See M. C. Smith (1984).

2. Caplow et al. 1982; and Caplow et al. 1983.

3. See Ratier-Coutrat (1982).

4. Caplow and Bahr 1989: 10.

5. See, for example, Caplow and Chadwick (1979).

6. See the article by Bahr (1987).

7. See the comment on the Middletown III project by Elder (1982).

8. Berger 1984.

9. See Roof (1984).

10. About this risk, see Smith (1984: 334).

11. Ibid.: 335.   12. As pointed out by Weales (1984).

13. De Tocqueville [1840–42] 1971.   14. Cofrancesco 1974: 37.

15. De Tocqueville [1840–42] 1971: 199.

16. About de Tocqueville's characterization of this aspect of early America, see Coldagelli (1990).

17. See Ferrarotti (1991).

18. See Baudrillard (1986).

CHAPTER 6. THE NINETIES IN MIDDLETOWN

1. Barbano 1983.   2. Bahr 1987.

3. See Caccamo (1991).   4. Bogg and Caccamo 1990.

5. Douglas 1986.   6. Ferrarotti 1991.

7. Bender 1978.   8. Stroppa 1987.

9. About "freaks" in American society, see Fiedler (1979).

10. As Baudrillard (1986) points out.

11. Caccamo 1996: 37.

Works Cited

Allen, Sheila, and D. Barker, eds. 1976. "Dependence and Exploitation." In *Dependence and Exploitation in Work and Marriage*. London: Longman.

Anderson, Elin L. 1937. *We Americans*. Cambridge, Mass.: Harvard University Press.

Anzieu, Didier. 1981. *Le corps de l'oeuvre*. Paris: Gallimard.

Bahr, Howard M. 1978. "Changes in Family Life in Middletown, 1924–1977." *Public Opinion Quarterly* 43, no 4.

———. 1982. "The Perrigo Paper: A Local Influence upon *Middletown in Transition*." *Indiana Magazine of History* 78 (March).

———. 1987. "Ups and Downs: Three Middletown Families." *Wilson Quarterly* (Winter).

Balbo, Laura. 1981. *Doppia presenza: lavoro intellettuale, lavoro per sé*. Milan: Franco Angeli.

Ball, Frank C. 1937. *Memoirs of Frank Clayton Ball*. Muncie, Ind.: [privately printed by] Scott Printing.

Ball, Moxley L. 1986. *Recollections of Lucina: The Best Years*. Indianapolis: [privately published].

Banfield, Edward C. 1958. *The Moral Basis of a Backward Society*. Glencoe, Ill.: Free Press.

Barbano, Filippo. 1983. "Marginalità vs complessità." In Sciolla Loredana, ed., *Complessità sociale e identità*. Milan: Franco Angeli.

Barnard, John D., and Donald F. Carmony. 1954. *Indiana: From Frontier to Industrial Commonwealth*. New York: Lewis Historical Publishing.

Baudrillard, Jean. 1986. *Amérique*. Paris: Grasset.

Bauman, Zygmunt. 1982. *Memories of Class: The Pre-History and After-Life of Class*. London: Routledge and Kegan Paul.

Beck, Ulrick. 1992. "How Modern is Modern Society?" *Theory, Culture, and Society* 9, no. 1: 163–69.

Bell, Colin. 1972. *Community Studies and Introduction to the Sociology of the Local Community*, New York: Praeger.

————. 1974. "Replication and Reality; or, The Future of Sociology." *Futures* (6 June).

Bell, Daniel. 1973. *The Coming of Postindustrial Society: A Venture in Social Forecasting*. New York: Basic Books.

Bell, Daniel, and Raymond Boudon. 1978. *Le contraddizioni culturali del capitalismo*. Turin: Biblioteca della Libertà.

Bellah, Robert N., Richard Madsen, William M. Sullivan, Ann Swidler, and Steven M. Tipton. 1985. *Habits of the Heart: Individualism and Committment in American Life*. Berkeley: University of California Press.

Bender, Thomas. 1978. *Community and Social Change in America*. New Brunswick, N.J.: Rutgers University Press.

Bendix, Reinhard, and Seymour M. Lipset, eds. 1966. *Class, Status, and Power; Social Stratification in Comparative Perspective*. New York: Free Press,.

Berger, Peter L. 1984. Review of *All Faithful People*. *America* (20 January).

Berger, Peter L., and Thomas Luckmann. 1966. *The Social Construction of Reality: A Treatise in the Sociology of Knowledge*. Garden City, N.Y.: Doubleday.

Berger, Peter L., Brigitte Berger, and Hansfried Kellner. 1973. *The Homeless Mind: Modernization and Consciousness*. New York: Random House.

Berger, Brigitte. 1981. "The Uses of the Traditional Sector in Italy: Why Declining Classes Survive." In Frank Bechhofer and Brian Elliot, eds., *The Petite Bourgeoisie*. New York: St. Martin Press.

Blumenberg, Hans. 1997. *Shipwreck with Spectator: Paradigm of a Metaphor for Existence*. Trans. Steven Rendall. Cambridge, Mass.: MIT Press.

Bogg, Richard, and Rita Caccamo. 1990. "Nei bar della provincia americana." *Politica ed economia* 10.

Borgatta, Edgar F., and Marie L. Borgatta, eds. 1992. *Encyclopedia of Sociology*. New York: Macmillan.

Bourdieu Pierre, J. C. Chamboredon, and J. C. Passeron. 1968. *Le metier de sociologue*. École Pratique des Hautes Études. Paris: Mouton and Bordas.

Bracken, A. E. 1978. "Middletown as a Pioneer Community." *Middletown III Project*, paper no. 10, Lynd Papers, Center for Middletown Studies, Bracken Library, Ball State University, Muncie, Ind.

Brady, Robert A. 1943. *Business As a System of Power*. Foreword by Robert S. Lynd. New York: Columbia University Press.

Caccamo, Rita. 1990. "Peter L. Berger: Il soggetto tra nomadismo e integrazione." In A. Izzo, ed., *Il ritorno del soggetto*. Rome: Bulzoni.

————. 1991. "Pro e contro il femminismo a Middletown: Un'indagine sul campo." *Memoria* 31: 127–42.

————. 1992. *Ritorno a Middletown: La provincia americana dai Lynd agli anni '90*. Rome: Bulzoni.

————. 1996. *Una sociologia e le emozioni: Helen Merrell Lynd (1896–1982)*. Milan: Franco Angeli.

————. 1997. "America anni venti: Il mutamento sociale nelle teorie e nelle ricerche." In E. V. Trapanese, ed., *Sociologia e modernità*. Rome: La Nuova Italia Scientifica.

Caillois, Roger. 1990. *L'incertezza dei sogni*. Milan: Feltrinelli.

Campbell, Colin. 1987. *The Romantic Ethic and the Spirit of Modern Consumerism.* Oxford: Basil Blackwell.

Caplow, Theodore H. 1979. "The Measurement of Social Change in Middletown." *Indiana Magazine of History* 75.

Caplow, Theodore H., and Howard M. Bahr. 1979. "Half a Century of Change in Adolescent Attitudes: Replication of a Middletown Survey by the Lynds." *Public Opinion Quarterly* 43, no. 1: 1–17.

———. 1989. "Middletown as an Urban Case Study." Unpublished manuscript.

Caplow, Theodore H., and Bruce A. Chadwick. 1979. "Inequality and Life Style in Middletown, 1920–1978." *Social Science Quarterly* 60, no. 3 (December).

Caplow, Theodore H., et al. 1982. *Middletown Families: Fifty Years of Change and Continuity,* Minneapolis: University of Minnesota Press.

Caplow, Theodore H., et al. 1983. *All Faithful People: Change and Continuity in Middletown's Religion.* Minneapolis: University of Minnesota Press.

Cavalli, Luciano. 1970a. *Il mutamento sociale: Sette ricerche sulla società occidentale.* Bologna: Il Mulino.

———. 1970b. *Introduzione a R. S. Lynd—H. M. Lynd, Middletown.* Vol. 1. Trans. Carlo A. Donolo. Milan: Edizioni di Comunità.

———. 1974. *Introduzione a R. S. Lynd—H. M. Lynd, Middletown.* Vol. 2. Trans. Carlo A. Donolo. Milan: Edizioni di Comunità.

Chase, Stuart. 1929. *Men and Machines.* New York: Macmillan.

———. 1931. "The Dogma of Business First." In Charles W. Thomas, ed., *Essays in Contemporary Civilization.* New York: Macmillan.

Chase, Stuart, and Frederick J. Schlink. 1934. *Your Money's Worth: A Study in the Waste of the Consumer's Dollar.* New York: Macmillan.

Click, P. C. 1947. "The Family Cycle." *American Sociological Review* 12.

Cofrancesco, Dino. 1974. "Tocqueville e il pensiero conservatore." *Controcorrente* 4 (October–December).

Cohen, Anthony P. 1985. *The Symbolic Construction of Community.* London: Tavistock.

Coldagelli, Ugo. 1990. *Introduzione a de Tocqueville, Viaggio in America, 1831–1832.* Italian trans. Milan: Feltrinelli.

Condran, John G., et al. 1976. *Working in Middletown: Getting a Living in Muncie.* Muncie, Ind.: Indiana Committee for the Humanities.

Coser, Lewis A. 1986. Introduction to *Knowledge for What? The Place of Social Science in American Culture,* by Robert S. Lynd. Middletown, Conn.: Wesleyan University Press.

Curti, Merle E. 1950. *An American History.* New York: Harper and Row.

———, ed. 1953, *American Scholarship in the Twentieth Century.* Cambridge, Mass.: Harvard University Press.

Curti, Merle E., et al. 1959. *The Making of an American Community: A Case Study of Democracy in a Frontier County.* Stanford, Calif.: Stanford University Press.

Dahl, Robert A. 1961. *Who Governs? Democracy and Power in an American City.* New Haven, Conn.: Yale University Press.

Dahrendorf, Ralf. 1959. *Class and Class Conflict in Industrial Society.* Stanford, Calif.: Stanford University Press.

———. 1967. *Società e sociologia in America*. Italian trans. Bari: Laterza, 1967.

De Tocqueville, Alexis. *La democrazia in America*. [1840–42] 1971. Trans. Silvano Tosi. Bologna: Cappelli.

Devereux, Georges. 1980. *De l'angoisse à la méthode dans les sciences du comportement*. Paris: Gallimard.

Dewey, John. 1922. "The American Intellectual Frontier." *New Republic* 10 (May).

———. 1929. "The House Divided Against Itself." *New Republic* 24 (April).

Dollard, John. 1939. *Class and Caste in a Southern Town*. New York: Harper and Row.

Douglas, Mary. 1986. *How Institutions Think*. Syracuse, N.Y.: Syracuse University Press.

Dreiser, Theodore. [1900] 1917. *Sister Carrie*. New York: Liveright.

Durkheim, Emile. [1902] 1966. The Rules of Sociological Method. Trans. Sarah A. Solovay and John H. Mueller. Ed. George E. G. Catlin. New York: Free Press.

Elazar, Daniel J. 1970. *Cities of the Prairie: The Metropolitan Frontier and American Politics*. New York: Basic Books.

———, ed. 1994. *Covenant in the Nineteenth Century: The Decline of American Tradition*. Lanham, Md.: Rowman and Littlefield.

Elder, Glen H. 1982. "A Third Look at Middletown." *Science* (21 May).

Elias, Norbert. 1988. *Coinvolgimento e distacco*. Italian trans. Bologna: Il Mulino.

Engler, Robert. 1979–80. "Knowledge for What? Indeed." *Journal of the History of Sociology* 2 (Fall–Winter): 122–26.

Etzkowitz, Henry. 1979–80. "The Americanization of Marx: *Middletown* and *Middletown in Transition*." *Journal of the History of Sociology* 2 (Fall–Winter): 41–57.

Featherstone, Mike. 1990. *Global Culture: Nationalism, Globalization, and Modernity*. London: Sage.

Ferrarotti, Franco. 1989. *La sociologia alla ricoperta della qualità*. Bari: Laterza.

———. 1991. *I grattacieli non hanno foglie: Flash americani*. Bari: Laterza.

Ferrarotti, Franco, E. Uccelli, and G. Giorgi-Rossi. 1959. *La piccola città: Dati per l'analisi sociologica di una comunità meridionale*. Milan: Edizioni di Comunità.

Fiedler, Leslie A. 1979. *Freaks: Myths and Images of the Secret Self*. New York: Simon and Schuster.

Flink, James J. 1972. "Three Stages of American Automobile Consciousness." *American Quarterly* 24: 86–87.

———. 1976. *The Car Culture*. Cambridge, Mass.: MIT Press.

Foucault, Michel. 1971. *L'archeologia del sapere*. Italian trans. Milan: Rizzoli.

Fox, Richard W. 1983. "Epitaph for Middletown: Robert Lynd and the Analysis of Consumer Culture." In R. W. Fox and T. J. Jackson Lears, eds., *The Culture of Consumption*. New York: Random House.

Frank, Carrolyle M. 1977. "Middletown Revisited: Reappraising the Lynd's Classic Studies of Muncie." *Indiana Social Studies Quarterly* 30.

———. 1979. "Who Governed Middletown? Community Power in Muncie, Indiana, in the 1930s." *Indiana Magazine of History* 75, no. 4 (December).

Freedman, J. I. 1978. *Happy People: What Happiness Is, Who Has It, and Why*. New York: Harcourt Brace Jovanovich.

Friedmann, Georges. 1946. *Problèmes humains du machinisme industriel.* Paris: Gallimard.

Freud, Sigmund. 1929. *Civilization and Its Discontents.* Vol. 21 of *The Standard Edition of the Complete Psychological Works of Sigmund Freud.* 24 vols. Trans. James Strachey. London: Hogarth Press, 1953–74.

Galbraith, John K. 1958. *The Affluent Society.* Boston: Houghton Mifflin.

Gale, Zona [1908] 1977. *Friendship Village.* New York: Ayer.

Gans, Herbert J. 1962. *The Urban Villagers: Group and Class in the Life of Italian-Americans.* New York: Free Press.

———. 1967. *The Levittowners: Ways of Life and Politics in a New Suburban Community.* New York: Vintage.

———. 1988. *Middle American Individualism: The Future of Liberal Democracy.* New York: Free Press.

Giannotti, Gianni. 1977. "Il concetto di comunità in Maine, Toennies, e Durkheim." *Rassegna italiana di sociologia* 4 (October–December): 525–57.

Giddens, Anthony. 1973. *The Class Structure of the Advanced Societies.* London: Hutchinson.

———. 1979. *Central Problems in Social Theory: Action, Structure, and Contradiction in Social Analysis.* Berkeley: University of California Press.

———. 1990. *The Consequences of Modernity.* Stanford, Calif.: Stanford University Press.

———. 1991. *Modernity and Self-Identity: Self and Society in the Late Modern Age.* Stanford, Calif.: Stanford University Press.

Goist, Park D. 1977. *From Main Street to State Street: Town, City, and Community in America.* Port Washington, N.Y.: Kennikat.

Goldberg, Vicki. 1986. *Margaret Bourke-White: A Biography.* New York: Harper and Row.

Goldthorpe, John H., et al. 1973. *Classe operaia e società opulenta.* Italian trans. Milan: Franco Angeli.

Gordon, Milton M. 1958. *Social Class in American Sociology.* Durham, N.C.: Duke University Press.

Gouldner, Alvin W. 1970. *The Coming Crisis of Western Sociology.* New York: Basic Books.

Halbwachs, Maurice. 1958. *The Psychology of Social Class.* Trans. Claire Delavenay. Glencoe, Ill.: Free Press.

Hannerz, Ulf. 1980. *Exploring the City: Inquiries Toward an Urban Anthropology.* New York: Columbia University Press.

Harrigan, John J. 1976. *Political Change in the Metropolis.* Boston: Little, Brown.

Hawley, Ellis W. 1970. *The New Deal and the Problem of Monopoly: A Study in Economic Ambivalence.* Princeton, N.J.: Princeton University Press.

Heer, Richard. 1962. *Tocqueville and the Old Regime.* Princeton, N.J.: Princeton University Press.

Herbert, O. 1970. *The American Family in Search of Future.* New York: Appleton-Century.

Hewitt, John P. 1989. *Dilemmas of the American Self.* Philadelphia: Temple University Press.

Hirschman, Albert O. 1983. *Felicità pubblica e felicità privata.* Italian trans. Bologna: Il Mulino.

Hofstadter, Richard, and Seymour M. Lipset, eds. 1968. *Sociology and History: Methods.* New York: Basic Books.

Hollingshead, August B. 1950. *Elmtown's Youth: The Impact of Social Classes on Adolescents.* New Haven, Conn.: Yale University Press.

Hoover, Dwight W. 1990. "Middletown Revisited." Ball State Monograph no. 34. Ball State University, Muncie, Ind.

Horkheimer, Max. 1947. *Eclipse of Reason.* New York: Oxford University Press.

Horney, Karen. 1955. *Neurosis and Human Growth: The Struggle Toward Self-Realization.* New York: Norton.

Hunter, Floyd. 1953. *Community Power Structure: A Study of Decision Makers.* Chapel Hill, N.C.: The University of North Carolina Press.

Hyman, Herbert H. 1954. *Interviewing in Social Research.* Chicago: University of Chicago Press.

Ilardi, Massimo, ed. 1990. *La città senza luoghi: Individuo, conflitto, consenso nella metropoli.* Milan: Costa and Nolan.

Izzo, Alberto, ed. 1977. *Storia del pensiero sociologico.* 3 vols. Bologna: Il Mulino.

———. 1991. *Storia del pensiero sociologico.* Bologna: Il Mulino.

Jensen, Richard. 1979. "The Lynds Revisited: Who Governed Middletown? Community Power in Muncie, Indiana, in the 1930's." *Indiana Magazine of History* 75, no. 4 (December): 301–19.

Kolko, Gabriel. 1962. *Wealth and Power in America: An Analysis of Social Class and Income Distribution.* New York: Praeger.

Kornhauser, Arthur W., ed. 1959. *Problems of Power in American Democracy.* Detroit: Wayne State University Press.

Laing, Ronald D. 1971. *The Politics of the Family and Other Essays.* New York: Pantheon.

Lasch, Christopher. 1977. *Haven in a Heartless World: The Family Besieged.* New York: Basic Books.

Lazarsfeld, Paul F. 1971. "Remarks Read at Memorial Service of R. S. Lynd." *American Sociologist* 6, no. 3.

Leuchtenburg, William E. 1963. *Franklin D. Roosevelt and the New Deal, 1932–1940.* New York: Harper and Row.

Lindberg, M. G. 1974. *The Incomplete Adult: Social Class Constraint on Personality Development.* Westport, Conn.: Greenwood Press.

Lingeman, Richard. 1980. *Small-Town America: A Narrative History, 1620–the Present.* New York: Putnam.

Lloyd, Craig. 1972. *Aggressive Introvert: A Study of Herbert Hoover and Public Relations Management, 1812–1932.* Columbus: Ohio State University Press.

Lowry, Ritchie P. 1965. *Who's Running This Town? Community Leadership and Social Change.* New York: Harper and Row.

Lynd, Helen M. 1945. *England in the 1880's: Towards a Social Basis for Freedom.* New York: Oxford University Press.

———. 1958. *Shame and the Search for Identity.* New York: Harcourt, Brace.

———. 1965. *Towards Discovery.* New York: Hobbs, Dorman.

————. 1983. *Possibilities.* Bronxville, N.Y.: Sarah Lawrence College, Friends of the Esther Raushenbush Library.

Lynd, Robert S. "Trip of Robert and Helen Lynd to Soviet Union in 1938." Typed Manuscript, Lynd Papers, Center for Middletown Studies, Bracken Library, Ball State University, Muncie, Ind.

————. 1921. "But Why Preach?" *Harper's Magazine* 113: 81–85.

————. 1922a. "Crude-Oil Religion." *Harper's Magazine* 114: 425–34.

————. 1922b. "Done in Oil." *Survey* 49 (November): 136–46.

————. 1924. "Lynd to Galen Fisher." Lynd Papers (carbon copy), Center for Middletown Studies, Bracken Library, Ball State University, Muncie, Ind.

————. 1934. "Why the Consumer Wants Quality Standard." *Advertising and Selling* 22.

————. 1936. "Democracy's Third Estate: The Consumer." *Political Science Quarterly* 60 (December): 486.

————. 1939a. *Knowledge for What? The Place of Social Science in American Culture.* Princeton, N.J.: Princeton University Press.

————. 1939b. "The Place of the University in 1940." *Columbia University Quarterly* 31 (December): 243.

————. 1945. "Planned Social Solidarity in the Soviet Union." *American Journal of Sociology* 51(November): 183–97.

————. 1950. "Ideology and the Soviet Family." *The American Slavic and East European Review* 9, no. 4 (December): 268–78.

————. 1951. "Our Racket Society." *The Nation* (25 August): 150–52

————. 1954. "Miscellaneous Items About Robert S. Lynd." *Journal of the History of Sociology* (March 3).

————. 1956. "Power in the United States." Review of *The Power Elite,* by C. Wright Mills. *The Nation* (12 May): 408–11.

————. 1957. "Power in American Society as Resource and Problem." In Kornhauser 1959.

Lynd, Robert S., and Helen M. Lynd. 1929. *Middletown: A Study in Modern American Culture.* New York: Harcourt, Brace.

————. 1937. *Middletown in Transition: A Study in Cultural Conflicts.* New York: Harcourt, Brace.

————. Papers. Manuscripts Division. Library of Congress, Washington, D.C.

Lynd, Staughton. 1979. "The Elk Basin Experience." *Journal of the History of Sociology* 2 (Fall–Winter): 14–22.

Madge, John. 1962. *The Origins of Scientific Sociology.* New York: Free Press.

Malinowski, Bronislaw. [1932] 1961. *Argonauts of Western Pacific: An Account of Native Enterprise and Adventure in the Archipelagoes of Melanesian New Guinea.* New York: Dutton.

————. 1966. *The Father in Primitive Psychology.* New York: Norton.

————. 1970. *Crime and Custom in Savage Society.* London: Routledge and Kegan Paul.

Mannheim, Karl. 1953. *Ideology and Utopia.* New York: Harcourt, Brace.

Marcuse, Herbert. 1968a. *Critica della società repressiva.* Italian trans. Milan: Feltrinelli.

————. 1968b. *L'uomo a una dimensione.* Italian trans. Turin: Einaudi.

Martindale, Don, and R. Galen Hanson. 1969. *Small Town and the Nation: The Conflict of Local and Translocal Forces*. Westport, Conn.: Greenwood Press.

Martinelli, Franco. 1974. *Le società urbane*. Milan: Franco Angeli.

———. 1981. *Società rurale e struttura di classe*. Milan: Franco Angeli.

Marty, Martin E. 1997. *The One and the Many: America's Struggle for the Common Good*. Cambridge, Mass.: Harvard University Press.

Mead, Margaret. 1949. *Male and Female: A Study of the Sexes in a Changing World*. New York: William Marrow.

———. 1971. *New Lives for Old: Cultural Transformation—Manus 1928–1953*. New York: Dell.

Merriam, Charles E. 1964. *Political Power*. New York: Collier.

Merton, Robert K. 1940. "Bureaucratic Structure and Personality." *Social Forces* 57.

———. 1955. Letter to Robert S. Lynd, 28 July. Lynd Papers, Center for Middletown Studies, Bracken Library, Ball State University, Muncie, Ind.

———. 1949. *Social Theory and Structure*. New York: Free Press.

———. 1980. Letter to Howard Bahr, 30 March. Lynd Papers, Center for Middletown Studies, Bracken Library, Ball State University, Muncie, Ind.

Mills, C. Wright. 1953. *White Collar: The American Middle Class*. New York: Oxford University Press.

———. 1956. *The Power Elite*. New York: Oxford University Press.

Mitchell, Wesley C. 1912. "The Backward Art of Spending Money." *American Economic Review* 2: 269–81.

Moore, Barrington. 1966. *Social Origins of Dictatorship and Democracy: Lord and Peasant in the Making of the Modern World*. Boston: Beacon Press.

Moore, W. E. 1963. "But Some Are More Equal Than Others." *American Sociological Review* 28, no. 1 (February).

Murdock, George P. 1949. *Social Structure*. New York: Macmillan.

Nelsen, Harry B. 1981. "Falling into the Future: Middletown in Decline." Sociology Research Centre, Ball State University, Muncie, Ind.

Nisbet, Robert A. 1957. *La communità e lo stato; Studio sull'etica dell'ordine e della libertà*. Milan: Comunità.

———. 1961. "The Study of Social Problems." In Robert K. Merton and R. A. Nisbet, eds., *Contemporary Social Problems*. New York: Harcourt, Brace.

———. 1969. *The Quest for Community*. New York: Oxford University Press.

———. 1981. *Sociologia come forma d'arte*. Italian trans. Rome: Armando.

Ogburn, William F. 1922. *Social Change with Respect to Culture and Original Nature*. New York: Bell.

———. 1928. *American Marriage and Family Relationships*. New York: Henry Holt.

———. 1930. Letter to Robert S. Lynd, 15 July (reply to letter from R. S. Lynd to W. F. Ogburn, dated 11 July 1930). Ogburn Collection, Joseph Regenstein Library, University of Chicago.

———. 1955. *Technology and the Changing Family*. Boston: Houghton Miffin.

Packard, Vance. 1958. *The Hiddens Persuaders*. New York: David McKay

Park, Robert E. 1924. "The Significance of Social Research in Social Life." *Journal of Applied Psychology* 8: 264–65. 1952.

———. 1955a. *Society*. Glencoe, Ill.: Free Press.

————. 1952. *Human Communities*. Glencoe, Ill.: Free Press.

Park, Robert E., Ernest W. Burgess, and Roderick D. McKenzie. 1925. *The City*. Chicago: University of Chicago Press.

Parrington, Vernon L. 1954. *Main Currents in American Thought*. New York: Harcourt, Brace.

Parry, Geraint. 1970. *Political Elites*. London: Allen and Unwin.

Parsons, Talcott. 1940. "An Analytical Approach to the Theory of Social Stratification." *American Journal of Sociology* 45 (November).

Perrigo, Lynn I. 1935. "Muncie and Middletown, 1923 to 1934." Ph.D. diss., University of Colorado.

————. 1938. "Community Background of Denver Criminality." *Social Forces* 17 (December): 232–39.

————. 1973. "The Process of Learning; or, The Tribulations of an Ordinary Professor." Unpublished autobiographical manuscript. Quoted in Bahr 1982.

Pizzorno, Alessandro. 1960. *Comunità e razionalizzazione*. Turin: Einaudi.

Plant, Raymond. 1974. *Community and Ideology: An Essay in Applied Social Philosophy*. London: Routledge and Kegan Paul.

Polsby, Nelson W. 1960. "Power in Middletown: Facts and Values in Community Research." *Canadian Journal of Economics and Political Science* 26 (November).

————. 1963. *Community Power and Political Theory*. New Haven, Conn.: Yale University Press.

Poulantzas, Nicos. 1975. *Classes in Contemporary Capitalism*. Trans. David Fernbach. London: New Left.

Radcliffe-Brown, Alfred R. 1952. *Structure and Function in Primitive Society*. London: Cohen and West.

————. 1957. *A Natural Science of Society*. Glencoe, Ill.: Free Press.

Ratier-Coutrat, Laurent. 1982. "Le programme de recherche sur Middletown III." *Sociologie du travail* 1 (January–March).

Redfield, Robert. 1955. *The Little Community*. Chicago: University of Chicago Press.

Riesman, David. 1950. *The Lonely Crowd: A Study of the Changing American Character*. New Haven, Conn.: Yale University Press.

Rivers, William H. R. 1906. *The Todas*. New York: Macmillan.

————. 1929. *Social Organization*. New York: Knopf.

Roof, W. C. 1984. Review of *All Faithful People*. *Science* (17 February).

Rosenberg, Morris. 1957. *Occupations and Values*. Glencoe, Ill.: Free Press.

Rossi, Peter H. 1963. "The Middle-Sized American City at Mid-Century." *Library Quarterly* 33.

Rothman, Robert A. 1978. *Inequality and Stratification in the United States*. Englewood Cliffs, N.J.: Prentice-Hall.

Salins, Peter D. 1997. *Assimilation, American Style*. New York: Basic Books.

Schlesinger, Arthur M. Jr. 1958. *The Coming of the New Deal*. Boston: Houghton Mifflin.

Schutz, Alfred. 1971. *Collected Papers*. The Hague: Martinus Nijhoff.

Shils, Edward. 1948. *The Present State of American Sociology*. Glencoe, Ill.: Free Press.

Sigfried, André. 1940. "Une grande enquete amèricaine." *Revue de Paris* 15 (April).

Simmel, Georg. [1903] 1957. *Die Grosstadte und das Geisteleben*. Stuttgart: K. F. Koelher Verlag.

Smith, Mark C. 1979–80. "Robert Lynd and Consumerism in the 1930's." *Journal of the History of Sociology* 2, no. 1 (Fall–Winter): 99–119.

———. 1984. "From Middletown to Middletown III." *Qualitative Sociology* 7 (Winter).

Sorenson, Helen. 1941. *The Consumer Movement: What It Is and What It Means*. New York: Harper.

Stein, Ben. 1979. *The View from Sunset Boulevard*. New York: Basic Books.

Stein, Maurice R. 1960. *The Eclipse of Community*. Princeton, N.J.: Princeton University Press.

Stoneall, Linda. 1983. *Country Life, City Life: Five Theories of Community*. New York: Praeger.

Stroppa, Claudio. 1987. *La pianificazione sociale: Teorie e metodi*. Rome: Bulzoni.

Suttles, Gerald D. 1972. *The Social Construction of Communities*. Chicago: University of Chicago Press.

Sylos, L. Paolo. 1974. *Saggio sulle classi sociali*. Bari: Laterza.

———. 1986. *Le classi sociali negli anni '80*. Bari: Laterza.

Tambo, David C., Dwight W. Hoover, and John D. Hewitt. 1988. *Middletown: An Annotated Bibliography*. New York: Garland.

Thernstrom, Stephan. 1964. *Poverty and Progress: Social Mobility in a Nineteenth-Century City*. Cambridge, Mass.: Harvard University Press.

Thomas, William I. 1923. *The Unadjusted Girl*. Boston: Little, Brown.

———. 1951. "Social Behaviour and Personality." New York: Social Science Research Council.

Tiévant, Sophie. 1983. "Les études de communauté et la ville: Héritage et problèmes." *Sociologie du Travail* 2 (April–June).

Toennies, Ferdinand. 1940. *Fundamental Concept of Sociology*. New York: American Book Co.

———. 1957. *Community and Society*. East Lansing: Michigan State University Press.

Treves, Renato. 1963. *Introduzione a Toennies*. Milan: Comunità.

Tumin, Melvin M. 1987. *Social Stratification: The Forms and Functions of Inequality*. Englewood Cliffs, N.J.: Prentice-Hall.

Turner, Frederick J. [1920] 1976. *The Frontier in American History*. Huntington: Krieger.

Vidich, Arthur J. 1980. "Revolution in Community Structure." In Art Gallaher and Harland Padfield, eds., *The Dying Community*. Albuquerque: University of New Mexico Press.

Vidich, Arthur J., and Joseph Bensman. 1958. *Small Town in Mass Society: Class, Power, and Religion in a Rural Community*. Princeton, N.J.: Princeton University Press.

Vidich, Arthur J., and Stanford M. Lyman. 1985. *American Sociology: Worldly Rejections of Religion and Their Directions*. New Haven, Conn.: Yale University Press.

Vidich, Arthur J., Joseph Bensman, and Maurice R. Stein. 1964. *Reflections on Community Studies*. New York: John Wiley.

Vitek, William, and Wes Jackson, eds. 1996. *Rooted in the Land: Essays on Community and Place*. New Haven, Conn.: Yale University Press.

Warner, W. Lloyd. 1959. *The Living and the Dead*. New Haven, Conn.: Yale University Press.

Warner, W. Lloyd, and Paul S. Lunt. 1941. *The Social Life of a Modern Community*. New Haven, Conn.: Yale University Press.

Warner, W. Lloyd, et al. 1963. *The Social Life of a Modern Community*. Vol. 1 of Yankee City Series. New Haven, Conn.: Yale University Press.

Weales, Gerald. 1984. "Welcome to Munciekin Land." *New York Review of Books* (26 April): 1–4.

Wheeler, Wayne. 1949. *Social Stratification in a Plains Community*. Minneapolis: [n.p].

Whyte, William F. 1943. *Street Corner Society*. Chicago: University of Chicago Press.

Wilson, William H. 1974. *Coming of Age in Urban America, 1915–1945*, New York: John Wiley.

Wissler, Clark. 1923. *Man and Culture*. New York: Thomas Y. Crowell.

Wolf, Stephanie G. 1976. *Urban Village: Population, Community and the Family Structure in Germantown, Pennsylvania, 1683–1800*. Princeton, N.J.: Princeton University Press.

Wrong, Dennis H. 1979. *Power: Its Forms, Bases, and Uses*. New York: Harper and Row.

Index

Library of Congress Cataloging-in-Publication Data

Caccamo de Luca, Rita.
    [Ritorno a Middletown. English]
    Back to Middletown : three generations of sociological reflections /
Rita Caccamo.
        p.   cm.
    Translation of: Ritorno a Middletown : la provincia americana dai
Lynd agli anni '90.
    ISBN 0-8047-3493-3 (cloth : alk. paper)
    ISBN 0-8047-3846-7 (pbk. : alk. paper)
    1. Muncie (Ind.)—Social conditions. 2. Muncie (Ind.)—Social
life and customs. 3. Lynd, Robert Staughton, 1892– Middletown. 4.
Lynd, Helen Merrell, 1896– I. Title.
    HN80.M85 C313 1999
    306'.09772'65—dc21   99-16822
                                                                  CIP
                                                                  rev.

⊗ This book is printed on acid-free, archival quality paper.

Original printing 2000
Last figure below indicates the year of this printing:
09   08   07   06   05   04   03   02   01

Typeset by Robert C. Ehle in 10.5/12 Monotype Bembo.